More Praise for *Fiercely You*

"*Fiercely You* is an inspiring book that provides a creative yet clever approach to being our most confident selves."

—**Anne Murray, Senior Director, Marketing Communications, Southwest Airlines**

"Who knew that the answer to women's problems with self-confidence would come from drag queens? Jackie Huba did—and she explains it all in her groundbreaking book, *Fiercely You*."

—**Liz Bullock, Director, Digital and Paid Media, Rackspace**

"*Fiercely You* is an inspirational book that takes the reader through a journey of self-discovery. The authors share strategies to eradicate self-doubt and embrace all aspects of life with authenticity, joy, and confidence, rather than fear and uncertainly. It's a must-read for all ages!"

—**Kathryn Ferguson, Senior Director, Marketing, SAP Americas**

"Jackie has done it again! She has turned drag queens into role models for every woman by making new and surprising connections. This is truly a guide that all women can use to build their own confidence and perform fearlessly in their many life roles."

—**Jennifer Hughes, Global Director, Social and Community, Electronic Arts**

"*Fiercely You* is your ticket to finding and setting free your playful, badass, bold, beautiful self. Step back, Jack. Jackie Huba's got one helluva ride for those who are ready to start expressing the version of themselves they've always wanted to be."

—**Victoria Labalme, performing artist, performance coach, and founder of Rock the Room**

"*Fiercely You* is for every woman who has ever daydreamed about what she should have done or said. This inspiring yet practical book provides an action plan on how to live your life with greater confidence."

—**Virginia Miracle, Chief Customer Officer, Spredfast**

"Hilarious and courageous, *Fiercely You* is the new how-to guide for women to build self-confidence and realize their true fabulous selves. Highly recommended!"

—**Gemma Craven, Senior Vice President, McCann**

"*Fiercely You* is a step-by-step powerful guide for women to learn how to be a force to be reckoned with. Using inspiring stories, Jackie and Shelly show us that we have the confidence inside to be whatever we want in this world. Just take the stage!"
—Kathie Jones, Global Controller, frog

"*Fiercely You* provides lessons anyone can take away on how to be strong, bold, fierce, and in control of your life, every day. It's a personal power development tool I would have loved to have had twenty years ago, when just starting my career."
—Stephanie Pfeffer Anton, Executive Vice President, Luxury Portfolio International

"A wonderful combination of a personal journey, glittering (and fierce) examples, sound research, and delicious process, Jackie Huba's *Fiercely You* provides women with a fun and fresh tool for building, growing, and leveraging confidence."
—Monique Maley, President, Articulate Persuasion, and creator of Command a Room Women's Leadership Program

"*Fiercely You* is an essential read for anyone seeking inspiration and guidance on how to stop worrying what other people think and start living boldly and vibrantly."
—Lyn Christian, MCC, CFCC, founder of SoulSalt

"*Fiercely You* is packed full of tips and advice to tap into your inner diva and become the fiercest, most confident version of yourself."
—Sarah Finley, cofounder and CEO, Social Arts & Science Institute

"Jackie Huba is a fearless role model for women who are holding themselves back from greatness. In this book, she shares the secrets to being the badass you always knew you could be."
—Amy Swank, Vice President of Operations, Texas Economic Development Council

"Like Sheryl Sandberg's *Lean In* wrapped in a feather boa, *Fiercely You* is a masterful and marvelous study of female empowerment in the modern age."
—Andrea France, retail software executive

"*Fiercely You* is an inspiring book that provides a creative and clever approach to being our most confident selves."

—Maxine Clark, entrepreneur

"Confident. Remarkable. Strong. Courageous. Who doesn't want that for themselves? I do. I know you do too. In *Fiercely You*, Jackie Huba and Shelly Kronbergs want to outfit you with a new way of seeing yourself in everyday situations. No bustier or thigh boots required!"

—Jill Silman, SPHR, SHRM-SCP, Senior Performance Consultant

"*Fiercely You* offers practical insights and creative tips and tools that can help you work through your fears and ignite your confidence."

—Barbara Miller, international speaker and speaking consultant/trainer

Fiercely
YOU

Fiercely
YOU

Be Fabulous and Confident by Thinking Like a Drag Queen

Jackie Huba
with Shelly Stewart Kronbergs

Berrett-Koehler Publishers, Inc.
1333 Broadway, Suite 1000
Oakland, CA 94612-1921
Tel: (510) 817-2277   Fax: (510) 817-2278   www.bkconnection.com

Ordering Information
Quantity sales. Special discounts are available on quantity purchases by
corporations, associations, and others. For details, contact the "Special Sales
Department" at the Berrett-Koehler address above.
Individual sales. Berrett-Koehler publications are available through most
bookstores. They can also be ordered directly from Berrett-Koehler:
Tel: (800) 929-2929; Fax: (802) 864-7626; www.bkconnection.com
Orders for college textbook/course adoption use.
Please contact Berrett-Koehler: Tel: (800) 929-2929; Fax: (802) 864-7626.
Orders by U.S. trade bookstores and wholesalers. Please contact Ingram
Publisher Services, Tel: (800) 509-4887; Fax: (800) 838-1149; E-mail: customer
.service@ingrampublisherservices.com; or visit www.ingrampublisherservices
.com/Ordering for details about electronic ordering.

Berrett-Koehler and the BK logo are registered trademarks of Berrett-Koehler
Publishers, Inc.

Printed in the United States of America

Berrett-Koehler books are printed on long-lasting acid-free paper. When it is
available, we choose paper that has been manufactured by environmentally
responsible processes. These may include using trees grown in sustainable forests,
incorporating recycled paper, minimizing chlorine in bleaching, or recycling the
energy produced at the paper mill.

Library of Congress Cataloging-in-Publication Data

Names: Huba, Jackie, author.
Title: Fiercely you : be fabulous and confident by thinking like a drag queen /
    Jackie Huba, with Shelly Stewart Kronbergs.
Description: Oakland, CA : Berrett-Koehler Publishers, Inc., 2016. |
    Includes bibliographical references and index.
Identifiers: LCCN 2016017377 | ISBN 9781626568075 (pbk.)
Subjects: LCSH: Self-realization in women. | Self-confidence. | Female
    impersonators—Psychology.
Classification: LCC HQ1206 .H777 2016 | DDC 155.2—dc23
LC record available at https://lccn.loc.gov/2016017377

First Edition
21   20   19   18   17   16   10 9 8 7 6 5 4 3 2 1

For **Rey Lopez, Kelly Kline,**
and **Jaremi Carey,** who so **generously**
shepherded me though my drag journey

—Jackie Huba

CONTENTS

SETTING SAIL FOR THE QUEENDOM

I hate cruises. So how is it that I found myself lying on a Swarovski crystal staircase in the middle of the night aboard the *Carnival Conquest* posing for a promotional photo for a drag performance and surrounded by a small entourage of inebriated drag queens? Ordinarily, I think of cruises as just too many people cooped up on a floating petri dish for a week. No ma'am Pam! But when I found out that there was such a thing as a "drag cruise," complete with forty of the country's top drag queens and twelve hundred drag aficionados from all over the world, I couldn't wait to sign up! My newfound love of drag knew no bounds. I couldn't find anyone crazy enough to go with me, so I had to book a cabin all by myself.

Every night of this five-night, six-day Caribbean cruise was a themed costume party. As an aspiring female drag queen (yes, women can do drag), I had been learning makeup and wig styling from my *drag mother** for a while at this point but still hadn't mastered it when it was time for the cruise. I felt intimidated, wondering about how I was going to do the wigs and makeup for my costume looks when these parties would be full of drag queens who were going to look *sickening*. I didn't want to go out looking like

---

* Drag culture has its own vocabulary. Drag terms will be italicized on their first usage in the text. You can find their definitions in the Glossary of Drag Terms at the end of the book.

an idiot. One of the last nights of the cruise was the Black Hearts Party, where the theme, of course, was to dress all in black. I was tired of looking so half-assed in my drag; my costumes were fierce, but my makeup and wig styling were awful, to tell the truth.

On the cruise, I met Phi Phi O'Hara, runner-up to the winner on Season 4 of *RuPaul's Drag Race,* the cult reality competition television show for drag queens hosted by the most famous queen in the world, RuPaul. Competing on the show when she was just twenty-five, Phi Phi was the young, talented spitfire queen, driven to win at all costs. Of course there is always drama on reality competition shows, and in her season of *Drag Race* Phi Phi was usually in the middle of it. In fact, she pulled so many shenanigans on the show that the *Huffington Post* put her on their "8 Nastiest Reality TV Villains" of the year list.[1] Not sure what to expect, I mustered up the courage to ask Phi Phi if she would help me with my makeup for the Black Hearts party. To my surprise, she immediately said yes! I'd remembered that my drag mother had told me I needed a promotional photo she could use in the online flyer for my performance during one of her upcoming shows. I didn't have one. I mentioned this to Phi Phi and she excitedly volunteered to help, saying: "I'll style your wig. I'll do your makeup. I'll direct the photo shoot. I'll Photoshop it. We'll have the photo done by the end of the cruise." I was dumbfounded. I had just met Phi Phi a few days earlier and here she was volunteering to do all of this for me. She seemed nothing like the bitchy character I'd seen on the show.

The night of the party, I brought my dominatrix-inspired outfit to Phi Phi's cabin: a black studded bra and corset, black high-waisted brief, black vinyl lace-up boots, fishnet hose, and a poker-straight, black shoulder-length wig with bangs. In the cabin she was sharing with her boyfriend Mikhael, it looked like her five giant pieces of luggage had exploded. There were costumes, wigs, high heels, makeup palettes, makeup brushes, eyelash glue, hairspray, and costume jewelry strewn around everywhere, even on the bed. It was hard to find a place to sit down. Phi Phi was in the middle of getting ready herself while at the same time working on another friend's makeup. She stopped to start working on mine. It was an honor to have such a professional *beat my face*. When I showed her the long straight black wig, she thought it would look better as a ponytail. She put my own hair in a tiny ponytail (my real hair is a short bob), and then worked some voodoo magic on the black wig—and voilà! It became a long ponytail that she attached on top of my own tiny one. Then she whipped out a can of black hairspray and began to spray all of my brunette hair black to match the new ponytail. Phi Phi remarked that there wasn't enough bling on my costume, so she lent me four giant sparkly, rhinestone cuffs, two for each wrist. With the look complete, I caught my reflection in the mirror. I didn't look anything like myself, but I looked sickening! For the first time, I felt like an actual queen. Lady Trinity, my drag alter ego, had come alive. The makeup and hair were impeccable, done by a seasoned professional. There were a number of the *Drag Race* queens at the costume party, and I took photos with a lot of them. Thumbing through the photos on my phone during the party, I remember thinking I looked as good as they did. All praise goes to Phi Phi!

Even at 3:30 a.m., after cocktails galore and a ton of dancing, Phi Phi hadn't forgotten about the photo shoot and was ready to go. She corralled a small crew of now sloshed people from the party and we made our way to the main lobby of the ship, where there were two stunning, curved, open-air staircases: one was made of clear steps filled with shimmering Swarovski crystals, and the other had shiny black stairs trimmed in sparkly white lights. At the top of the Swarovski crystal staircase, Phi Phi directed me, "OK, go down and lie on those stairs." Um, what? I made my way to the vertical center of the staircase and awkwardly tried to strike an attractive pose, legs outstretched and crossed, my left hand on my hip. The whole crew hung over the railing above, just looking at me. I tried another pose, putting my hand up by my head and pinning what I hoped was a seductive look on my face. But I felt like I just looked stupid. All of a sudden I felt stone-cold sober, so instead of experiencing an alcohol-induced brazenness, I just felt really insecure.

I was intimidated by Phi Phi because she is a master at modeling for photos, as many drag queens are. She knows how to pose. She knows angles. She knows lighting. Phi Phi again tried to direct me, "No, softer face. Softer face!" I didn't even know what the hell that meant! She tried again, "Just open your lips a little." Dammit! I felt so inept. I'm sure I looked like a dork. Then Phi Phi directed again, "Grab your ponytail and hold it straight out to the side, real sexy-like." Real sexy-like? Was she kidding? I felt so vulnerable with everyone above the railing staring down at me. At that moment, a ship maintenance guy who was walking by started catcalling. Oh great! Exactly what I needed.

Phi Phi wasn't completely happy with the shots from this staircase so she suggested we go to the black staircase nearby and start the whole process all . . . over . . . again. It was all so awkward. I had no experience with modeling like this. I felt so dense and self-conscious because I didn't know how to pose. It was really nerve-wracking. Somehow we completed the shoot with no one in our crew guffawing at my awkward poses or faces. At 4:15 a.m., we all headed to our rooms for the night with my early-morning drag queen supermodel photo shoot complete. OK, well, maybe not so super.

I ran into Phi Phi at lunch the next day and she told me she was already done with the photo. Apparently she had stayed up until 5:00 a.m. to pick out the best shot and Photoshop it. Wow! I went back to her room after lunch to get a copy of the image. When she showed it to me, I was dumbfounded. At first, I couldn't find any words. The photo was just stunning. I couldn't believe it was me. In it I'm a

Lady Trinity's first promotional photo
(Photo by Phi Phi O'Hara)

vixen, posing seductively on the black stairs, looking hot as shit. Holy hell, I looked amazing! Especially for a forty-eight-year-old woman. I mean, hot damn!

This became the promotional photo I have used for all of my drag performance gigs. In fact, I blew the image up into a $3' \times 4'$ poster, framed it, and it's hanging on my bathroom wall right now, so I can see it every single day. I use it to remind myself of how awesome I am. I don't say that with arrogance; I say it with pride. That photo reminds me of the first time I was able to see an image of myself as a powerful woman. I know that if you want this feeling, that moment will come for you too, when even if you aren't doing drag, you will realize that you can pull off big changes within that reflect your fiercest self. I guess you could say that cruise was my coming out in drag. It was the first time that Lady Trinity had been fully realized as a character, an alter ego. Phi Phi O'Hara made Lady Trinity come alive, and I will always have her to thank for this. I like to think of her as my "drag aunt," though we have never formalized the role. Honestly, I'm just grateful to be able to call this sweet, generous, sarcastically funny, extremely talented, and hardworking person my friend.

Before this cruise, I had lived a so-called normal life. I was an ex-IBMer, ex-corporate executive, author, and middle-aged woman in her late forties. But my love and reverence for the art of drag and the performers who are transformed by it has changed my life. And choosing this path to become a female drag queen has been one of the most terrifying and rewarding choices I have ever made. I learned how to do drag from some of the best drag queens on the planet. From these queens I also learned how to be the most fabulous and confident version of myself in everyday life. Doing drag has bestowed upon me strategies to manage my self-esteem issues, helped me to take myself less seriously, and enabled me to live my life more boldly. In short, I now own my own power. And I love it! You too can feel this amazing and fierce, and you don't need to do drag to do it. All you need to do is just *think* like a drag queen in your everyday life. OK, well maybe wearing a few more sequins wouldn't hurt either.

PART ONE

WHY FIERCE MATTERS

The Need for Fierce

When was the last time you did something that astounded those around you, that amazed yourself, that was outside of your comfort zone? Has it been a while? Was it in your childhood, or at college? If it was recent, did you need the help of a drink or two to muster up that courage? That's pretty common. But when was the last time you felt intimidated, insecure, afraid to do something because it might be wrong? Or when was the last time you watched someone else do something bold and you thought, "That's amazing! But I could never do that?" Unfortunately, that's pretty common too. Why? Fear. We often hold ourselves back from our true potential because of all kinds of fears—fear of failing, fear of rejection, fear of being laughed at, and even the fear of being our most glorious self.

This lack of confidence shows itself most measurably in our work lives, especially in women as compared to men. In a study by Hewlett-Packard, women working at the company applied for promotions only when they believed they met 100 percent of the qualifications necessary for the job. The men were happy to apply when they thought they could meet 60 percent of the job requirements. The study showed that women felt confident only when they feel perfect.[1] A 2014 U.S. gender parity study at Bain & Company looked at employees' career aspirations and their confidence in getting a top management position. Both men and women were equally confident about their ability to reach a top management position at the start of their careers. However, over time, women's aspiration levels dropped more than 60 percent while men's stayed the same. As they gained experience, women's confidence also fell by half, while men's stayed about the same.[2] As both of these studies demonstrate, we women are holding ourselves back from our professional goals and aspirations because of our lack of confidence.

Marianne Williamson, a celebrated spiritual teacher, author, and lecturer, directly addressed this issue when she wrote:

> Our deepest fear is that we are powerful beyond measure. It is our light, not our darkness that most frightens us. We ask ourselves, Who am I to be brilliant, gorgeous, talented, fabulous? Actually, who are you *not* to be? You are a child of God. Your playing small does not serve the world. There is nothing enlightened about shrinking so that other people won't feel insecure around you. We were born to manifest the glory . . . that is within us.[3]

So let's release these inhibitions and fears in order to be the fabulous people we imagine we could be. What would your life be like if you could actually become that dazzling diva you dream of being? It would be shinier than all the sequins on a stage full of drag queens, that's what! It would be more powerful than all those nagging, negative voices that live with you and inside your head.

What would it be like to live your life boldly, vibrantly, barely giving notice to those inner and outer voices that constantly harangue you to step back, quiet down, and not take that risk? Imagine for a moment, though, what would happen if you and all the people you know were set free from their fears and were able to embrace a life of exuberance. Can you feel that energy simmering? That spark of excitement, of possibility, is actually power, plain and simple. It is the new meaning of an old word that is changing, and that word is FIERCE.

The *Oxford English Dictionary* still defines "fierce" as "having or displaying an intense or ferocious aggressiveness."[4] Violence is implied. It has been a bloody word, often used to refer to battle. But the word "fierce" is in the process of morphing into something else, something more refined. The *Urban Dictionary* serves up several definitions of "fierce," such as "having exceptional quality, being bold, displaying chutzpah, cool, and eye-catching," and being used to describe someone "who is on fire and possesses too much swag for the common man or woman to handle."[5] As we see it, the word "fierce" means bold, empowered, confident, fabulous, remarkable, outspoken, and strong. We want a world that's full of this kind of fierce. We want our friends to be fierce. We want you to be fierce.

And we've found a way to do that. We've found the fiercest collection of people on the planet, and we want to share with you what we have learned from them so that you can be your most fabulous and confident self by thinking like they do.

Ladies and gentlemen, we give you . . . THE DRAG QUEENS!

Learn from the Queens of Fierce

So just how *does* a middle-aged ex-IBMer, ex-computer programmer, former corporate executive, author, and straight woman go from that to performing in drag as the glamorously fierce Lady Trinity? Here's how it all started.

Raised in a blue-collar family, I (Jackie) did everything I could to be the best daughter possible: I got straight As in school, behaved perfectly, earned a degree in computer science, and became a hardworking marketer at IBM. I was always the good girl, doing the right thing, never making waves. I did fine but never felt good enough. After a failed marriage and another failed long relationship, I started to question who I was. I wrote two marketing books with my former significant other and became a successful management consultant and speaker. When that relationship/professional partnership ended I found myself on my own, in my forties, at the lowest point in my life. I was bored with the work I had been doing, felt stifled creatively, and knew I wasn't living up to my potential. I felt insecure and knew something drastic needed to happen. At forty-seven, though, I wasn't sure that I had the confidence to reinvent myself and do something completely different. I was stuck.

During this time, not coincidentally, I found myself freakishly drawn to and inspired by pop superstar Lady Gaga. She even became the subject of my third, and first solo, business book, *Monster Loyalty: How Lady Gaga Turns Followers into Fanatics*. Here was a woman who had created a powerful, disruptive persona—complete with crazy makeup, big wigs, wild costumes, and tall heels—and had successfully conquered the misogynist, male-dominated recording industry.

I began to think, doesn't everyone, every day, create personas as we act out the various roles we play in society? You have a professional persona you create for work, a more nurturing persona with your kids, a free-spirited persona when you are out with your friends, and I could go on and on. All of these personas together make up our personality. But in adult life we often alter our personas too much in order to fit into society. We worry about what others will think of us. Sometimes it's just easier to conform rather than stand out. This is especially true for women. Psychology tells us that self-doubt derails us from pursuing our passions and accomplishing our greatest goals. Fear and doubt keep us clinging to conformity and stop us from being our best selves.

And, sure enough, there I was one night in my every-day uniform—a wrap dress with comfortable (and, I'd later learn, dowdy) slingbacks, alone, feeling defeated on the couch, surfing through channels when I stumbled on *RuPaul's Drag Race*. I simply could not keep my eyes off of those drag queens I was seeing on the screen. Here were men going balls out (or, more precisely, in) to create these fierce, fabulous, female characters for the stage. I watched them, envious, as they unabashedly transformed themselves into whatever their hearts desired, unafraid to flout the socially acceptable boundaries of beauty by experimenting with costumes, cosmetics, and wigs that defied expectations and even gravity. Here were men revering womanhood and pulling together the most feminine, most fabulous, and most glamorous traits that I (supposedly) just naturally possessed. No limits, no apologies, just strong, bold, dynamic femininity accessorized with a stiletto-sharp wit and a give-no-fucks attitude. As I watched season after season of the show, I began to realize that drag queens are terrific role models for how to build confidence: they create bold personas, own the way they look, command attention using powerful body positions, aren't afraid to take risks, and can shake off criticism with a flip of their wig. When I found myself in challenging personal and business situations, I started thinking, "What Would a Drag Queen Do?" I wondered how I could live every day with that sense of empowerment.

"What Would a Drag Queen Do?"

Something that RuPaul said really changed my thinking about how I could attain the same confidence as the queens I watched on the show. She said, "You're born naked and the rest is drag."[1]

Most of us think of drag as being a performance art for the stage. But RuPaul's insight is that we create and *perform* personas in our everyday life. Whether you know it or not, you are doing drag right now. You do drag every day. Your drag is not just what you wear, but also how you act, what you say, how you say it, and how you carry yourself. And we can transform ourselves into any persona we want, just as we did when we were kids on Halloween. What I wanted was the power and confidence of the drag performers I saw on TV. Hell, if men could make this

"You're born naked and the rest is drag."

amazing transformation into fierce glamazons through drag, why couldn't I? So while still doing my day job, I decided that I, Jackie Huba, would become—wait for it—a drag queen!

As I mentioned earlier, women can do drag. When most people think of drag performers, they think of men performing as female characters who are, of course, called drag queens. Actually, there are other lesser-known categories of drag: women who perform in drag as male characters are called drag kings, and women who do drag as female characters are known as bio-queens, faux queens, or simply female drag queens. That's what I wanted to do.

I began to immerse myself in the world of drag. I watched hundreds of live drag performances, went on two drag cruises, interviewed the world's top drag queens about how they create their powerful female personas, and got their advice on how to do the same for myself. Many of the queens I interviewed have been on *RuPaul's Drag Race,* because in the drag world these performers represent the best of the best. I interviewed Courtney Act, Derrick Barry, April Carrión, Adore Delano, Laganja Estranja, Miss Fame, Cynthia Lee Fontaine, Jujubee, Trixie Mattel, Chad Michaels, Coco Montrese, Phi Phi O'Hara, Raven, Latrice Royale, Yara Sofia, Shangela Laquifa Wadley, and Katya Zamolodchikova.

I mentored with a local drag mother; developed my own drag persona named Lady Trinity; learned how to do theatrical makeup, wig, and costume styling; mastered the art of lip-syncing; and learned to playfully seduce my audiences (large and small). I've performed in some of the top drag events in the world. And I've met multitudes of others who've also been transformed by their love of drag queens, some of whom are profiled in this book. I want you to be transformed the way they were.

An Invitation to Be Fiercely You

This is your chance, your opportunity to make a change. You are reading this book because you long for something more. You want to be more *you*. You are tired of hiding the shiny, sparkly parts of yourself because of the fear of criticism. You want to experience the feeling of being your most fabulous self. You want to be confident, strong, full of life. This book will show you how to do it—how to be *fiercely you*.

Fiercely You is the culmination of what I (Jackie) have learned from the world of drag. It is a personal growth guide to help you ignore criticism, live life more fearlessly, and become the fierce and fabulous creature you may dream of being every day by learning lessons taught by drag queens. It will offer advice from other people who have been transformed by using drag queens as role models and will trace my personal experience of diving into the Queendom.* My collaborator, Shelly Stewart Kronbergs, will dissect and explain how the lessons we can learn from drag queens are rooted in well-researched concepts in psychology. Everyone, meet Shelly!

Hello, darlings! I'm Shelly, and here are the letters after my name: MDiv, MA, LMFTA. Let me break that down for you: master's degree in divinity from a Lutheran seminary. I was ordained as a minister in the Evangelical Lutheran Church in America and was the pastor of a wonderful old

---

* We are using the term "Queendom" to refer to an enlightened worldview in which we see ourselves as confident and fearless as seasoned drag queens.

country church outside of Austin, Texas. Next is the master of arts degree in counseling, with a dual track for both LPC and LMFT. Those letters stand for licensed professional counselor and licensed marriage and family therapist, but I chose to go the LMFT route and am currently licensed as an associate in that field.

All of these letters and degrees may impress you and assure you that I just might know what I'm talking about. Or maybe they'll just bore you—I'm OK with that, too. What the letters don't show you is that I, too, am fully engaged in becoming fiercely me, and I want to share with you why this book works. Because it does. And the reason why it works is that its premises rest on strong psychological foundations. The book is more than merely anecdotal, it is supported by scholarly research on the psychological issues of power, the structure of personality, the construction and performance of our identity, and the ways in which change can be produced in our lives. It is a privilege for me to provide that information for you and to help you become the person you dream of being.

Thanks, Shelly! Now let's get started! In this book you will find the five Keys to Fierce that will unlock your inner fabulousness and help you think like a fierce drag queen in your everyday life. They are:

1. **Create Your Drag Persona.** Consciously create the person you've always wanted to be.

2. **Always Look Sickening in Everyday Drag.** Dress for power.

3. **Strike a Pose and Embody Your Power.** Use power posing and physicality to instill inner confidence.

4. Tell Your Critics to Sashay Away. Quiet both inner and outer critics.

5. You Better Werk! Take small risks to propel yourself to taking even bigger ones.

These keys unlock the wisdom that will set you free: **you get to control who you are in this world.** Too many of you feel controlled by your significant others, your bosses, your friends, your children, your parents. You feel that you need to fulfill their expectations of you. You succumb to the perceptions you *think* they have of you—perceptions that you aren't smart enough, pretty enough, strong enough, capable enough. We want you to consider less what other people think and instead focus on becoming who you were meant to be. Only *you* can let out that inner queen who is confident in herself no matter what other people think. Only you can create the amazing person you see inside your head and feel in your heart.

The next five chapters will break down in detail the five Keys to Fierce. Each chapter has a similar format that looks like this:

- An explanation of each key.

- How Jackie and her drag alter ego, Lady Trinity, experienced this key.

- *Notes from the Stage:* insights and advice from top drag queens on this key.

- *Notes from Everyday Queens:* profiles of real people who are shining examples of how this key has worked for them.

- *Notes from the Couch:* proven psychological research that supports how this key improves confidence levels. Shelly will break down the research into layman's terms and explain the science behind why these keys really work.

- *Notes for Your Drag Diary:* specific homework assignments to help you personalize each key. The "Drag Diary" is where you record your thoughts, fears, excitement, and progress of working through each key. The "diary" could be any place you want to record your thoughts: a paper notebook, the notepad on your phone, and so on. It's important to write down your progress so that you can reflect back on the new things you have tried and be inspired by your past accomplishments.

By the way, these are not just suggestions. We want you to connect with those people who *do* see your potential and make them a bigger part of your lives, so they can cheer on your accomplishments and remind you of how fabulous you are when you are feeling less than confident. We want to form a community to make this change. That's why we are introducing the **"50 Days to Fierce Challenge!"** Gather your like-minded friends, either as a book club, a meet-up, or in our online community through our website, EnterTheQueendom.com. Post your efforts on social media for the world to see and support. Change can happen. It's all within your control. Because remember, as RuPaul said, you are already in drag. You can create a powerful, confident persona that is fiercely you just by deciding to do it.

An important note as we move forward: we are not suggesting that to gain these benefits of feeling fabulous and more confident you need to actually become a drag queen. The idea here is to take the ways that drag queens create fierce, bold personas and apply them to our everyday lives to create self-confidence. But in order to apply them, we can't just change our *thinking*; we have to change our *actions*. You will be asked to do things that you may never have done before, things that might make you feel silly, or embarrassed, or uncomfortable. Things that might push your boundaries. Of course, you are still in control of what you do, and nothing you are asked to do will be untoward. There are ways to incorporate a fabulous new you without breaking a dress code at work. Shelly even has a story about wearing stiletto heels under her clergy robe! The big idea here is that when we push ourselves, even just a little, to *do* things outside our comfort zone, we *feel* liberated, as though we can take on something else we feel afraid of. Taking action makes us feel more confident. That said, in the Drag Diary sections of the keys, we will prescribe advanced activities for those who are "drag curious," that is, who want to have a more adventurous drag experience.

It is also important at the outset to clear up any confusion about the differences between drag queens, transvestites, transgender people, and cross-dressers. Umbrella terms like "transvestite" and "cross-dresser" mean dressing and acting in a style or manner traditionally associated with one's opposite gender. But there are many reasons why someone might be acting or dressing as the opposite gender. "Drag queen" usually connotes cross-dressing for the purposes of entertainment and self-expression. Some people, usually heterosexual men, cross-dress to fulfill transvestic fetishes; that is, their cross-dressing is primarily part of a private sexual activity. "Transgender" is the state of one's gender identity not matching one's assigned sex at birth.

Some drag queens are also transgender women. This can be confusing. Some men who are questioning their gender identity are attracted to drag because it allows them to explore their female side. After these men transition to female, some continue to perform because they love the stage and entertaining a crowd. To put it simply, for transgender drag queens, drag is what they do, but trans is who they are.

Don't know much about drag queens? The history of drag is long, storied, and important to know. Sashay your way to this book's "A Drag Primer: Know Your *Her*story," and you'll learn about drag queens' historic role in the fight for LGBT (Lesbian, Gay, Bisexual, Transgender) rights, detailed explanations of the various styles of drag, and examples of drag in modern pop culture. Know your drag *her*story!

And, finally, a word on gender pronoun usage in this book. In the drag world, when we are referring to a male drag queen dressed in drag, we use the pronoun "she." When we are referring to the same male person out of drag, we use the pronoun "he."

Would you like to have a powerful, confident inner drag queen that you can access any time you feel insecure? Can you imagine the power that can reside inside you as a fierce alter ego? Are you ready to create your own drag persona that will empower you to face the challenges in your life? Do you want to see how both drag queens and everyday people of all ages have used their alter egos to change their lives for the better? Then get ready to take the first step into the Queendom! Follow us for a road map of how to craft your own fabulous, fierce persona!

PART TWO

THE KEYS TO FIERCE

The First Key

....

CREATE YOUR DRAG PERSONA

“ *Drag doesn't change who you are, it actually reveals who you are.*”

—RuPaul[1]

RuPaul Andre Charles is a 6′4″, fifty-five-year-old African American man. But when he is dressed as "the Monster," as he affectionately calls himself in drag, he is transformed into an even taller, stunning, female glamazon.[2] How tall? "With hair, heels, and attitude . . . I'm through the mother-freakin' roof!" he says, in classic RuPaul style.[3]

Though RuPaul uses his actual first name as his drag name, his female alter ego is a completely different character from his everyday self. For RuPaul and other drag queens, creating an alter ego or persona goes beyond just the outward transformation achieved by wigs, makeup, and costuming. Queens are creating a whole new character, which they express as a separate disparate identity from their everyday selves. Sometimes you will hear queens refer to their characters in the third person. Their drag characters are often completely different in personality from the person behind the facade. The drag character sometimes is used to compensate for perceived flaws in the performer's own identity; for others, it can serve as a conduit for personal expression. April Carrión, a talented twenty-six-year-old drag queen and art student from Puerto Rico, told me: "April for me is more than a character. She's a blank canvas. . . . I just see [her] as a never-ending project as just being who I want to be. . . . I love her, and with her I like to experiment in so many different ways, in my makeup and my hair, my clothes, just everything."[4]

This idea that you can be anything you want in drag is so different from what we experience in our everyday lives, especially for women. We have roles we play—as a working woman, as a parent, as a spouse, as a daughter—and most of us mold our everyday personas to fit those roles. Sometimes it's just easier to conform, because otherwise we have to deal with the consequences of standing out. Those consequences may be judgment in the form of verbal criticism, untoward looks, exclusion, or even ostracism. Perhaps this is why so many women are drawn to the fearlessness of drag queens. Fun fact: from the start of *RuPaul's Drag Race* Seasons 1 through 8 (the last season as of this writing), the audience demographics have always been 50 percent women. One of those women is Courtney Constable, a twenty-six-year-old female drag queen from Toronto, Canada, who just happens to have a master of arts degree in women's and gender studies and is a professional writer when not in drag. Her drag persona's name is Courtney Conquers, and her drag style is extremely diverse. She explains the idea of becoming the image of her imagination through the art of drag.

> You can *literally* be anything you want. I've dressed as a raver, a barbie doll, an alien, a supermodel, a paper cutout, a bride, various animals, and any other number of things that I've never actually been. Sure, I could wear those costumes without "doing drag," but drag is more than just the outfit. It's the confidence, attitude,

and beliefs that go along with it. I'm not just a barbie doll; I'm a sparkly barbie doll who also happens to be witty, smart, hilarious, and thinks she's, like, *really* good at dancing. Drag is like playing adult pretend, only you're doing gender activism just by standing there looking like that. . . . What adult *doesn't* secretly want to spend their weekend transforming themselves into literally anything their mind can think of? The ones who say they don't are liars.[5]

Now imagine *you* could start with a blank slate and create the person you have always wanted to be. Someone who would try things you are afraid to try, do things you are scared to do, wear things you wouldn't dare to wear, and say things you would never say. Can you see this person in your mind's eye? Who is it? Can you imagine a fully realized persona that is everything you've always wanted to be? Creating this powerful alter ego and alternate persona is the mechanism this book uses to enable you to conceptualize and then actualize the amazing person that is inside you. Let's look at how female entertainers, drag queens (including Jackie), and even an eighty-seven-year-old great-grandmother have created their drag personas so that you can learn how to do this too.

Dolly, Gaga, and Beyoncé: Other Bold Broads in Drag

Women in entertainment have long been adopting over-the-top, bold personas. Many performers have a persona that emerges when they take the stage, but Dolly Parton, Lady Gaga, and Beyoncé have more in common with drag queens than they do with other actors or singers. They've created distinct female characters different from their everyday personas, sometimes with a completely different name and identity. Often they'll use wigs, costuming, and makeup to construct this character. The character may have a distinctive voice and mannerisms that are more pronounced or exaggerated on stage.

Country singing superstar Dolly Parton may have kept her real name as her stage name but her signature look is borrowed from the town tramp. Born dirt poor and having to wear homemade feed-sack dresses in a small Tennessee town, Parton never idolized glamorous female movie stars because she never was exposed to them. She never got to go to the movies or read fashion magazines. The only pretty girls she saw were the models in the Sears & Roebuck catalogue. So it's not surprising that Dolly was captivated by the local town prostitute, whom she described as "all glamour [with] the red nails, the red toenails, the high heels, the short skirt, the pretty legs, the big hair." Dolly remembered: "She was breathtaking to me. It was very striking. And that's how I wanted to look."[6] As a young girl, Dolly felt unattractive and plain. She said the way the local prostitute looked reflected her innerself and gave her the courage to turn that into her stage persona.[7] While she's been nipped and tucked a bit over the years to hone her self-described "trashy" look, she loves the persona she has created. "My image is over-the-top—my clothes are as tacky as Graceland, but it's helped me to be recognized all over the world. I have no taste or style and nobody cares. I love it."[8] In fact, she admits that her look is so over-the-top that "it's a good thing I was born a girl, otherwise I'd be a drag queen."[9]

In 2006, a twenty-one-year-old, 5'1" singer-songwriter named Stefani Joanne Angelina Germanotta made a name for herself by creating the Lady Gaga persona, complete with crazy makeup, big wigs, wild costumes, and tall heels. She did this to conquer the misogynistic recording industry when she was first starting out. "What I went through in the business. . . . I was just a little girl from New York in a very male-dominated industry. It's very scary. It was really intense. It changed me not in a good way. It made me hard, and it made me kind of vacant and insecure. That's when I started to put on all of the wigs and put on all of the outfits, because it was through transformation that I was able to free myself of those insecurities. I was able to become somebody else."[10]

In 2011, when Gaga lobbied President Obama to make bullying a hate crime, she had the chance to speak with the president in person at a fund-raiser later that year. She knew she needed to exude real power; she was meeting with the leader of the free world, for Pete's sake! After the meeting, President Obama joked to the press that he'd found Lady Gaga "intimidating" because "she was wearing sixteen-inch heels and was eight feet tall."[11] Well, maybe they weren't exactly sixteen-inch heels, but we're guessing they were high enough to make her taller than the president. Inhabiting her over-the-top persona, she brilliantly used her wardrobe to create a powerful impression and get her message across.

Beyoncé Knowles may be a mega-pop star now, but she started out with her two best girlfriends performing for the ladies under the hair dryers at her mother's beauty salon. The three girls called themselves Destiny's Child, performed as teens in the talent show circuit, and eventually landed a recording deal with Sony. "I always held back in Destiny's Child, because I was comfortable in a group and felt that I didn't have to do anything a hundred percent, because there were other people onstage with me. I would not lose myself or go all the way," Knowles told *Vanity Fair* in 2005.[12]

A Houston, Texas, native, Knowles was born into a religious household and grew up singing in the Methodist church. How did she go from a shy member of a young girl group to a bold solo diva singing about how she is the "female version of a [hustler]"?[13] She created a more sensual and outspoken persona, called Sasha Fierce, in order to be more confident and to perform sexy, aggressive songs outside her comfort zone. "I have someone else that takes over when it's time for me to work and when I'm on stage, this alter ego that I've created that kind of protects me and who I really am."[14] Beyoncé says the inspiration for Sasha Fierce came from the drag-house circuit in the United States, an unsung part of black American culture where working-class gay men channel ultra-glamour in mocked-up catwalk shows.[15] What all of these female entertainers have in common—both on the stage and in life—with drag queens is the confidence their alter egos have given them. They have embraced the powerful feeling that comes from being someone different and the freedom and strength their onstage personas provide them.

Becoming Lady Trinity

When I (Jackie) decided to do drag, one of the very first things I had to do was develop my drag character. This included coming up with a name and a style or aesthetic. This is an extremely daunting task. Where do you start? As a writer, the best way to describe it is: I got "drag character development block"! I could be anyone I wanted to create, but who *did* I want to be? Perfectionist that I am, I wanted to get it right the first time. I didn't want to be that queen who starts performing under one name and then later switches to another; I was afraid that would be confusing and diminish my power. But I was comforted by the advice of seasoned Las Vegas–based drag queen Coco Montrese: "Remember this, there's no right or wrong when it comes to drag. Drag is the most open profession, hobby, whatever it can be. It's the most open thing. There's nothing you can do wrong."[16]

Lots of drag queens have names that are puns or use a clever form of wordplay. Anna Mosity, Rhea Listic, Clara Tin, Anita Cocktail, and Lauren Order are just a few. These are fun, but I wanted to choose a name that had more meaning to me. To start the naming process, I first began thinking of attributes I wanted my drag character to have. I wrote down: classy, fearless, confident, sleek, precise, complex, sexy—all things I wanted to be but wasn't pulling off in my real life. Then I thought about what movie characters I have been drawn to in the past. My favorite movie of all time is *The Matrix* (but not the two sequels; they suck). I love *The Matrix* for its lead female character, Trinity, played by Carrie Ann Moss. Trinity is a computer hacker who has escaped from the Matrix where she was imprisoned by sentient machines. She is a kind of superwoman. Master of kung fu fighting and a skilled shooter, she can take out a roomful of gun-wielding enemies without displacing a single hair. She is an equal partner with her male counterparts in the mission to defeat Agent Smith and the machines. I love that Trinity is a steely badass who can hold her own with the male characters but also exudes sexiness. In the movie, she possesses a quiet intensity, confidence, and power. She isn't bombastic or loud. Her costumes in the movie are always skin-tight, black, and usually vinyl or latex. She reminds me of a nerdy dominatrix in her shiny black catsuit and black boots.

So I chose Trinity as the name for my character. But something was missing. The name needed a second word. I thought about which other women or female characters I had connected with and one name kept coming up: Lady Gaga. I had been studying her for over five years for my first solo book. She is fierce, fabulous, and confident—everything I wanted to be. I decided to combine "Lady" from Lady Gaga with Trinity to get Lady Trinity. I loved it!

But my friends didn't. I shared the name with them and they thought it was just okay. I started to second-guess my choice. My friend Cameron, a fellow drag queen aficionado, started brainstorming names that he thought were more like the character attributes I had come up with earlier. He suggested names like Veronique Stark, Bella Donna, and Veronica LaCroix. They were dark, sexy names, and perhaps could be those of beautiful burlesque dancers. But I just wasn't feeling it. The name Lady Trinity just had too much meaning for me. Not wavering from my choice was my first real act of power—a nod to the Trinity I was to become. I was—no, *am*—Lady Trinity.

It wasn't until the first time I put on the thigh-high boots, *Dynasty*-shouldered jackets, glamorous long, wavy wigs, and bold makeup, though, that Lady Trinity came alive for me. She felt powerful. As Jackie, I was someone who often worried about what people thought of me. Lady Trinity is different from the Jackie I was at the time. I often doubted myself, as many women do. For example, I remember deeply doubting myself when writing my previous book on Lady Gaga. Who in hell would want to read an entire business book with a crazy pop star as the main case study? It took me months to really commit to writing it. I decided I was going to have to self-publish it because I thought no publisher would be interested. Ultimately it was acquired by Portfolio, an imprint of Penguin Books and the top business book publisher in the industry, right before I was about to self-publish it. And it has been a huge success. But I wasted months ruminating on whether to even write it in the first place.

Lady Trinity, however, believes in herself. She has the balls to perform in drag in nightclubs along with experienced queens. She knows that she is fierce and fabulous and doesn't hesitate to wear something skimpy or provocative that most middle-aged women wouldn't be caught dead in. She is supremely confident. She doesn't listen to the haters. She will do what she wants and is not concerned if others don't like it. She's not rude, but she won't take any crap from anyone. Lady Trinity has the qualities that I've always wanted to have. And now that I have her as a part of me, I can call her up, in and out of drag, and channel her confidence and fierceness.

How an *American Idol* Alum Overcame His Insecurities by Becoming Adore Delano

Before he began doing drag, Danny Noriega had already had a brush with fame. He is a gifted singer from Azusa, California, and made it to the semifinals on *American Idol* in 2008 when he was just seventeen years old. Noriega is a master at creating characters, and post-*Idol* he became a YouTube star, creating skits as a self-described *"chola"* (a tough, street-savvy Latina) character known as Angel Baby. In 2011,

Adore Delano
(Photo by Magnus Hastings)

Noriega began performing in the Los Angeles clubs as his drag persona, Adore Delano. He says the basis for the punk rock–styled Adore are women he admired while growing up, including his mom and misunderstood beauties from Hollywood like Courtney Love. But the alter ego of Adore is more than just thick black eyeliner, ripped fishnets, and Budweiser bodysuits. Noriega says Adore is his superhero. "I was bullied really bad in elementary school, in the middle school, and some high school. In a way I put the makeup on and the facade back then even. . . . After *American Idol*, when I picked back up the makeup, and I was going to the clubs and performing, it was like, 'I found my voice. I found my confidence again.' It's almost like a shield of any fucked-up shit that happened."[17]

Noriega's Adore character has also allowed him to overcome insecurities brought on by a father who never approved of his sexual orientation. "When I was seven, he said that basically he was embarrassed by me because I was feminine and I liked girl things. And it really stuck with me, and I think that has a lot to do with my confidence [issues]. . . . A lot of my insecurities come from that."[18] Noriega told me in an interview, "I feel, in a way, Adore really does mask [those insecurities] and grabs the bull by its balls and takes over, [she] doesn't give a shit."[19] As with Danny, our drag persona can be our superhero too, imbued with special powers that can be called up when we need them. All we have to do is will her to appear.

Baddie Winkle:
The Eighty-Seven-Year-Old Raver

"I've always been a rebel all my life. When somebody tells me I can't do something I'm going to show 'em I can."[20] Helen Van Winkle may have always been a rebel, but she's never looked this good. Reinventing herself in her late eighties as her alter ego Baddie Winkle, this great-grandmother was recently named by *Cosmopolitan* as

Helen Van Winkle, aka Baddie Winkle, on the
red carpet at the 2015 MTV Music Video
Awards
(Photo by Jordan Strauss/Invision/AP)

one of the Internet's Most Interesting People.[21] The neat thing about Baddie—and what seems to resonate most among her 1.7 million Instagram followers, 430,000 Facebook fans, and 221,000 Twitter followers—is her refusal to conform to society's standards of what an eighty-seven-year-old should look like. Her favorite color is neon pink. She is fond of fake fur boleros and brightly colored tie-dyed T-shirts with sayings like "Booty is love" and "Will commit sins 4 Chipotle." She also rocks bathing suits, crop tops, and brightly colored hair.

Until recently, life for Helen hadn't been so rosy. She lost her husband on their thirty-fifth anniversary in 1983 and her military-serving son in 1999. "I blamed God forever," Helen recounts. "I cried all the time because I couldn't come to terms with it, so I made myself over into Baddie Winkle."[22]

One day Helen was spending time with her nineteen-year-old great-granddaughter Kennedy. In her silver pixie haircut, she decided to try on some of the teenager's clothes—a tie-dyed shirt and a pair of cutoff shorts. Kennedy, thinking great-grandma looked hip and cute in the clothes, took a photo and posted it to her Instagram account. The photo got so many reposts and comments that Kennedy suggested to her grandmother that she should start her own Instagram account. They came up with the screen name Baddie Winkle and Helen's sassy, badass alter ego was born. Baddie's Instagram bio simply reads, "Stealing your man since 1928."

Baddie, with Kennedy's help, began posting photos on Instagram in psychedelic, teen-influenced clothes. Baddie says she doesn't like "old women" clothes: "I never wore them in my life."[23] She believes that dressing for one's age is complete bunk: "I don't feel old. I have never felt old. I think you can dress any way you want to."[24]

After pop stars Rihanna, Miley Cyrus, and Drake started following her on social media, designers from around the world began sending Baddie clothes. Los Angeles–based hip clothing designer Dimepiece (a favorite of Rihanna) created an ad campaign with Baddie as the star. The sassy senior was styled and photographed wearing the label's signature streetwear, including mesh tunics and sexy swimsuits, lounging by a sunlit pool sipping on a Miller Lite. Dimepiece said it selected Baddie for the campaign because she proves that "you're never too old to be the baddest bish in the room." (In case you were wondering, "bish" is slang for bitch, but used in a playful sort of way.)[25]

The octogenarian social media sensation has gone from hashtags to Hollywood. Baddie appeared on an episode of the reality show *Candidly Nicole* with Nicole Richie and walked the red carpet at the premiere of *Orange Is the New Black* Season 2, posing with the show's stars. But perhaps the most buzz-worthy thing to happen to Baddie was being invited to the 2015 MTV Video Music Awards by the show's host, Miley Cyrus. Miley had been a huge fan of Baddie, previously posting one of the Dimepiece ads on Instagram with a caption calling her "a badass role model for all of us!!!!!!"[26]

Creating her badass alter ego Baddie Winkle has helped Helen not only to get over her grief but also to rekindle her sense of self and add more fun and creativity to her life. "Baddie Winkle has helped me a lot—in spirit, anyway. The lesson I have learned is live and let live," she says. "I would love to be a role model for older people. You're only here once in your lifetime, so have fun."[27] Baddie Winkle is Helen's drag persona, and it has helped her gain a new lease on life. And by adopting a fierce persona that allows her to experience all of the colors in the crayon box of this world, she's not just a role model for "older people" as she says. She's a role model for all of us!

 FROM THE COUCH

The Psychology of Gender Performativity and Fabulation

Let's talk about alter egos, personas, confidence issues, questions of identity, gender performance, and fabulation. It's a lot to unpack so I (Shelly) will break it down. Let's start with the persona. All people have a persona, in fact multiple personas. This is not to be confused with the disorder of having multiple personalities! A personality is the inner psyche's structure: its mannerisms, interests, and abilities that each person has inside. The persona, though, is how we present ourselves to the world. The word "persona" derives from a Latin word meaning "mask." It is not a literal mask, but represents all the diverse social masks that we wear in different groups and situations. For instance, a woman will exhibit one persona at her child's parent–teacher conference—probably that of a concerned, responsible mother—and then don an entirely different persona when she goes out on the town that evening with her old friends from college—perhaps a younger, rowdier, wilder version of herself. This is perfectly normal. We all do this, usually quite seamlessly. The folks who deny this and say, "Oh, I'm just always me. What you see is what you get. I'm the same yesterday, today, and tomorrow," have plenty of mental health experts calling that bullshit! In fact, my first thought would probably be, "Well, now, what are you trying to hide from me, and from yourself?"

According to Carl Jung, one of the founding fathers of psychology, the persona is a public sense of self, the self that an individual displays to the world. Everyone has multiple personas, but if you believe that the persona is *all* that your personality is composed of, you might be too adjusted to the outer world and not enough to your inner world.[28] You might tend to believe that you are nothing more than the image you project outward to the world, and that that is all you need to be. The truth is that we are complex people who need both an inner identity and an outer image. And this is why drag works so well.

This complexity is evident when you step into a situation that is new or challenging when you aren't certain what to do, and your subconscious is unsure which inner or outer persona to assume. For instance, the respectful, dutiful employee persona rarely works in a roomful of older, male colleagues who have merit badges in "mansplaining" whom you are tasked to lead in a committee meeting. Neither will the self-effacing, compliment-devaluing, "Why can't I lose ten pounds?" persona work when one is making an important speech in front of a roomful of academic peers. These are situations that call for something much stronger and bolder. These circumstances require a persona that is courageous—a persona that is fierce enough to ignore criticism yet playful enough to engage everyone in the room in a positive way. A persona that allows that gloriously fierce you to shine.

This is where the term "fabulation" comes in. Fabulation (by the way, I love this word!) usually refers to a way of writing that uses fantasy or fantastic elements; but Dickie

Beau, a talented London actor and drag performer, or "fabulist," uses this term to refer to art that "projects into the world images that are so intense they take on a life of their own."[29] You see, if you are going to be your fiercest self, you need to develop a persona that is intensely fabulous. Because it is this intensity, this over-the-top quality, that allows your persona to take on a life of its own and to become fully real for you. Only then can you call on it in your everyday life to help you manage those confidence-jarring situations.

The good news is that this fierce and fabulous queen-like persona is already present somewhere in your psyche. And believe it or not, she fits well inside you. If you are one of those naturally sweet, bubbly people, then there is a good chance that your inner queen resembles Glenda, the Good Witch from *The Wizard of Oz*. Or there is also the possibility that an extremely sweet, bubbly nature has been suppressing a slightly naughtier persona, maybe one with a more acerbic tongue, and vice versa. If the personas of motherhood, the good wife, and the quiet, grateful daughter are starting to feel a bit heavy, then it may be time to give voice to the inner stripper, or even to the inner whip-wielding dominatrix. The important thing, though, is to create this persona so that she balances out the other personas, so that she does not create too much dissonance inside. She needs to feel like she could be you if only you were bold enough. She is definitely that friend who pushes you when you need it. She needs to feel fun, exciting, and invigorating, because she can bring you the confidence and power that you have been longing for!

This is more than just a fun exercise. The great news about this whole process is that it has the power to create a permanent change deep within you. A study at Stanford University showed that a modest intervention, just one small step, that helps to change beliefs about one's ability to change, has the power to make permanent, positive changes to a person's personality structure and functioning.[30] This means that the process of developing a new, strong persona that you believe can change you, and that you then experience as a positive, liberating event, can actually bring about a lasting change in your life.

In fact, the whole notion of performing, especially as someone other than the self you tend to project to the world, has its own dedicated field of study. It's called "performativity," which is often linked with social constructionism, and some really educated and powerful thinkers have a lot to say about it. Foremost in the field is Judith Butler, a philosopher, author, and professor at the University of California–Berkeley, who posits that gender is not who you are, what your body indicates, or a category that society puts you in, but rather is simply *what you do*. It is your actions—your performance, if you will—that determines who you are. And one of the key places where this is most evident is in the drag culture. Drag queens choose the gender, identity, and persona of the character that they assume, and in doing this, they become it. They reconstruct their own identity.

Still have some doubts? Not quite sure if it's possible that a fabulated persona has the power to make you fabulous? Hang on, because another study published in the journal *Personal Relationship* found that when people with waning self-esteem wrote down the positive qualities they saw in their favorite same-sex celebrities *and* themselves, they felt closer to their ideal selves. That is, these imaginary relationships with people they don't know (also called parasocial relationships) can benefit people because they feel more confident just by thinking about the qualities of people they admire.[31]

So if you admire the fearlessness of drag queens you can literally feel more fearless just by thinking about them. Picture your fierce, fabulous self. Admire her. Imagine yourself in that role. Because thinking about it has the power to change you. This is part of the process of internalizing and becoming fiercely you, and this is why it works!

 FOR YOUR DRAG DIARY

Bringing Your Alter Ego to Life

Drag queens do it. Pop stars do it. Even eighty-seven-year-old great-grandmothers do it. They create bold, confident personas that they can call forth when they need them. Now it's time for you to craft your own everyday drag persona. Yes, we know this might seem a little weird. Trust us. In order to really call up this persona, we need to make her real. At the end of this exercise, we will have a name for your persona, an aesthetic, and a description of her personality traits.

Get out your Drag Diary and get ready to write. Date the top of the page, as this will help track your progress. Then write down answers to the following prompts.

1. Remember a specific time when you felt like your most confident, badass self. Copy down these sentences and fill in the blanks: "I remember a time when I was a real badass. When I felt the most badass, I was _____ years old. I was _____ [describe what you were doing] and I felt like _____ [describe how you felt].

2. Visualize your most confident future self. How do you want to be? List three to five words that describe this future self.

3. Make a list of three to five women you admire and who have some or all of the badass feeling and confident qualities that you listed in Steps 1 and 2, respectively. These can be real women who are historical figures from the past, current figures in politics, celebrities, professors, and so on. They can also be female characters in movies, TV shows, or books. Actually, who says they have to be women? They can also be male versions of any of the above. Circle one or two people for whom you have the most affinity. Choose one or two attributes from each one and write them down.

Now let's start to visualize your drag persona.

4. In your Drag Diary, open to a new page. If your Drag Diary is electronic, get a piece of blank paper and something to write with. Close your eyes. Yes, close your eyes. Now draw the first thing that comes to mind when you think of your drag alter ego. Don't think too much about it. Just draw what comes to mind.

5. Now open your eyes and add some details. Just let it flow, like you did in the margins of your seventh-grade notebook when that teacher was droning on and on and on . . .

6. Picture that gorgeous creature and write down some descriptions of what she looks like. What color is her hair? What does she wear? Is she a

punk? Is she glamorous? Serious or silly? For the overachievers, start a Pinterest page and pin the shit out of her until that character is clear in your mind.

7. Carry her around for a while in your heart. Before you go to sleep tonight, resolve both to dream about her and to remember the dream.

8. Let's think now about her name. There's no perfect way to pick a drag name. It's best to think of some words that could be in the name and then combine them in different permutations until you find one that resonates with you. Here are some tips:

    (a) Write down some of the names from Step 3 that you like.

    (b) Write down words that describe what you drew in Step 5.

    (c) Create various combinations of words and names.

    (d) Narrow these down to a few that you like and say them out loud. Which ones roll off the tongue better than others?

9. Share your best names with your friends and ask for their feedback.

10. Let the list alone for a few days and then come back to it. Which name keeps standing out as your favorite? That one is your winner!

11. If absolutely no drag name appeals to you, then there's always the tried-and-true method: make

the first name that of your favorite pet and the last the name of the street you grew up on.

Make sure to share your drag name with us on social media by tagging @jackiehuba on Twitter or Instagram with #FiercelyYou.

Note for our Drag Curious readers:

- Google your drag persona's name to make sure there aren't a whole lot of other queens with the same one.

- Grab the social media accounts for your drag persona's name ASAP before someone else grabs them! Then you won't have to deal with TheLadyTrinity as your Instagram name like I do because someone already has LadyTrinity. Doh!

Condragulations! Now you have a fierce, bold, confident persona with an identity that is fiercely you. It's a name you will be able to access later when you need to boost your confidence. When you feel afraid to take an action, you will say, "Now what would [insert your drag name here] do right now?" And then you'll do exactly that!

Now that we have started the creation of your everyday drag persona, we are going to move on to another key to fierce: how to dress for power. Would you like to know why what you wear on the outside makes you feel powerful on the inside? Then let's keep going!

The Second Key

ALWAYS LOOK SICKENING IN EVERYDAY DRAG

❝ *I firmly believe that with the right footwear, one can rule the world."*

—Bette Midler[1]

Five wigs stitched together to make one giant three-foot-tall beehive wig; size 16 floor-length hand-beaded gown; rhinestone pumps with seven-inch heels; a tearaway cape made out of feathers—for drag queens and their costumes, nothing is too big, too outrageous, or too over-the-top. Drag queens are experts at using wigs, clothing, shoes, and accessories in the most imaginative ways to create their magnetic personas. They dress to command attention. They strut onto the stage with attitude, and the audience gets caught up in all the fabulousness they exhibit. Worcester, Massachusetts–based drag star Joslyn Fox explains: "I think a big part of the reason people love drag queens is because of the confidence they instill in people. When people see a queen on stage there's that part of them that thinks, 'If they can do it, I can do it,' and that gives them that confidence to go ahead and wear that hot pink lipstick to school, or to go ahead and wear those fishnets under that skirt and feel sexy at work. Drag allows people to feel confident in expressing who they are."[2] Now we know that you aren't going to drag it up big-time for the office, but you can take a cue from queens about how to focus on the outside so you feel more confident and powerful on the inside.

Have you ever stood in your closet and thought, "These clothes aren't me?" Have you yearned to change your wardrobe into something . . . more?—more vibrant, more bold or colorful? Into something that makes a statement about who you really are? But have you given up because you didn't know how to go about it? Well, hang on, because this is where we show you how! How to create that look, how to translate the power styling of drag queens with their wigs and makeup and shoes into something that makes you feel fiercely you!

Red Lipstick and Jumpsuits: How a Stylist Helped Overcome Everyday Drag Fears

Remember Garanimals? It's a line of children's clothing separates, introduced in 1972, that makes it easy for kids to choose coordinated outfits by themselves by picking pieces with matching hang-tags. (By the way, they still exist.) See, I (Jackie) have always been a Garanimals-type of gal when it comes to fashion. I've never been good at putting outfits together. When I found something I liked (shirt/pants/shoes), I would buy each item in three colors and then mix and match to make outfits.

Well, in March 2013 (way before Lady Trinity had emerged), I was preparing for a summer book tour for my new book on Lady Gaga. I had joined a small startup consulting company, and I really hadn't been doing speaking engagements for the previous two years. As I surveyed my closet, I realized I had nothing to wear on my book tour. Shit! I couldn't go on stage talking about Lady Gaga in this boring corporate-y wardrobe. I spied one somewhat fashionable dress: a classic Diane von Furstenberg wrap dress with splotches of forest green and brown. Pair that with some low-heeled black patent leather slingbacks and bam!—new speaking uniform. Now all I had to do was go to Nordstrom and get four more wrap dresses and a few more pairs of slingbacks, each a different color, and I'd be all set.

At Nordstrom, I was at the register with my armful of colorful new wrap dresses when I realized that I still didn't really know how to put these together. What color shoes went with these dresses? What jewelry would be best to accessorize with? Should I get a new handbag? I mentioned this to the clerk, and she said, "You know, we have stylists here at Nordstrom, and they're free." A human Garanimals matcher! And it cost nothing. Bonus!

Two weeks later I came back to the store for my appointment with Irene Scott, one of their best stylists. I brought my four wrap dresses, in various colors. I brought my three identical pairs of slingbacks, in various colors. Into the dressing room walked a smiling woman in her mid-forties, with a sleek brunette bob haircut, dressed impeccably in skinny black pants with a strip of leather going up the sides, a tailored black jacket with white-and-black calfskin lapels and black suede high-heeled ankle boots. I commanded: "Irene, here is what I need. I've got my four dresses. I've got my three pairs of shoes. I just need to know how to put this together. So if you could just help match jewelry, maybe a bag, I'll be set."

"Ohh-kayy," Irene said slyly, bringing her hand to her chin and slowly cocking her head slightly to one side. From that utterance I wasn't sure what she was thinking, but it couldn't be good.

"Put on one of the dresses with a pair of the shoes and let's take a look." Dutifully, I did what Irene said. When I walked out of the dressing room, she didn't mince words: "Well, I wouldn't let my grandmother wear those shoes. I know they're expensive and Italian, but that heel height is too dowdy for you. And that dress? Meh."

I was stunned. Did she just insult me? Did she realize that I had *actually gone on stage* wearing the same dress and shoes that she'd just disparaged? Did I really look that bad on stage? Why hadn't anyone told me this outfit was so dowdy? She went on: "I Googled you. You wrote a book about Lady Gaga, right? And even based on my interaction with you just now, I can tell you that this outfit is not right for you. It's not who you are. You are *fiercer* than that."

Wait. What? For some reason, everything in the dressing room just seemed to freeze in time. I literally had goose bumps. Had I heard her right? She'd just called me . . . fierce.

Gobsmacked by this word, I just stood there speechless. Not having anything to say is not normal for me. I'm not sure anyone had ever called me fierce, at least not to my face. And here was a woman I barely knew who had said she could see this quality in me. How did she see this in me when I wouldn't describe *myself* that way? Oh my gosh, really? Am I . . . fierce? I mean, Lady Gaga is fierce. Drag queens are fierce. But am *I* fierce? Well I guess if she believed it, there might be a kernel of truth there. Maybe I am fierce. I'm fierce! I. AM. FIERCE. The idea started to sink in that maybe, just maybe, she was right. What should I do now?

"Just hold on," Irene said. "Let me go grab some things." Fifteen minutes later, she was back with her arms full of clothes and shoeboxes. She began to hang the clothes up around the dressing room: a sleeveless black wool asymmetrical-hemmed dress, a navy blue leather jacket, slim-cut black pants with leather panels on the front, black suede ankle boots, and more. I must have had a really skeptical look on my face. "Trust me," Irene said. "Just try them on."

So I did. And I couldn't believe what I saw. I looked like I'd just walked out of a fashion shoot for *Vogue* in New York City. Or maybe I'd just walked out of a record company's office in L.A. having signed a contract for my new album. It was someone else. It was someone who looked . . . amazing. Could this be the fierce me that had been inside there all along?

"Now this is really you, right? I love you in all of this!" Irene said after I had tried on almost everything in the room. "So I have one more thing for you. Look at this. It's a designer jumpsuit." She pointed to a one-piece garment that incorporated a sleeveless top and pants. If you've never seen one, it's like a onesie for women, only more fashionable. This particular jumpsuit was black with a white dotted pattern and wide pants that tapered in at the ankles. They reminded me of MC Hammer pants.

I said to Irene, "I'm sorry, I really liked everything else that you brought in. But *that?* That is a clown suit. Kim Kardashian would wear that. I would *never* wear that." Reassuringly, with a sly smile, Irene told me that not everyone could pull this off, but she thought I could. I put the jumpsuit on and I guess it looked okay, but damn those pants! Who the hell wants big billowy pants around one's hip area? She paired the jumpsuit with a hip black suit jacket and the black ankle boots. She convinced me that we should go down to the ladies' shoe department, while I was still wearing the outfit, to pick out some better shoes to go with the ensemble. As we walked out of the dressing room and toward the escalator, I seemed to be catching the eyes of fellow shoppers and store employees, and they were checking me out. On the escalator, people going up turned their heads, and their eyes followed me as I went down. A Nordstrom employee we passed stopped me and excitedly wanted to know who had put this outfit together for me. I pointed to Irene, who was smiling like a Cheshire cat. In the ladies' shoe section, an exuberant shopper came up to me, pointed at the outfit, and just exclaimed, "Wow!" Sold!

Great. So now this crazy woman had convinced me to buy every single thing I tried on. I made space in my closet for the "fierce clothes." A month went by and I hadn't worn any of them. None. Nada. Was this stuff really me? I didn't know anymore. Every day when I got dressed in my old clothes, I would see the price tags still on the stuff from Nordstrom. The tags screamed at me, reminding me how much it had all cost. I really needed to at least *try* to wear some of this stuff soon; or maybe I'd just take it all back. I was already halfway through the book tour and hadn't worn *any* of it. What a coward!

Disgusted with myself, I decided to take a chance at my next event, a keynote speech for a large marketing conference in Las Vegas. I packed the black asymmetrical sleeveless wool dress and gray peep-toe suede pumps for the stage and decided to give that damned onesie jumpsuit a try at the reception the night before. Irene had also told me to wear red lipstick with the jumpsuit ("It's a MUST!"). I'd *never once* worn red lipstick in my entire life. I didn't wear red lipstick—red is so bright and just screams, "Look at my mouth!" Well, if I was really going to do this, then MAC Russian Red lips it had to be.

At the event at the MGM Grand Hotel, I nervously entered the evening reception wearing my new jumpsuit, my red lipstick, the black blazer, and black suede peep-toe pumps. I was a bundle of nerves. Did I look like a Kardashian wannabe? There were about two hundred marketing directors from large corporations in a cavernous ballroom, and I gingerly approached a small group sipping cocktails around a tall table. "Hi. I'm Jackie Huba, your keynote speaker for tomorrow."

After a round of great-to-meet-you's, I will never forget what happened next. A fifty-ish woman in a corporate business suit walked around the tall bar table and approached me, only stopping when her face was just inches from my own. In a low forceful voice but with a beaming grin, she whispered, "You. Have. Balls."

Seeing the confused look on my face, she pointed at my outfit and said, "That." Then she repeated a little louder, "You. Have. Balls." Bam! Now someone else was acknowledging that so-called fierceness I was supposed to have. In that moment it finally dawned on me that maybe it's in there. Maybe it had been in there all along, and this act of wearing something outside my comfort zone had brought it to the surface. I now understood that I could own my own power and that looking the part helped me do it. This outerwear was helping me become the fierce woman that I'd seen glimpses of over the years but had mostly kept inside.

I've never worn anything from my old wardrobe since that aha moment. Irene has since helped me to overhaul everything from business wear to casual wear, including jewelry, purses, footwear, and coats. I've replaced my *entire* wardrobe, and now my clothes match my new fierceness. There is lots of leather, some sequins, and even fashionable

Before

After

(Photos by Mira Budd Photography, David Heisler, Tina Hodnett)

thigh-high suede boots. Some of it reminds me of what a drag queen might wear at her office job! The above pictures show the overhaul of my everyday drag look.

Quick note on Irene: she's now an independent stylist living in Seattle, Washington, and you can find her at IreneStyling.com.

Mastering Makeup, Wigs, Costumes, and, Thank God, No Tucking

Around the same time that I met Irene, I had become friends with the kingpin of drag entertainment in San Antonio, Texas, Rey Lopez. For a year, I had been driving the seventy-five minutes from Austin to Rey's monthly drag shows because he was booking the queens from *RuPaul's Drag Race* to perform. They were celebrities to me and I wanted to see them live. San Antonio had been a hotbed of drag for decades, and after a bit of a decline, Rey was bringing his city back to the forefront of the national drag scene. He booked the best queens that San Antonio had to offer as part of his shows: the hilarious Tencha La Jefa as the host, and as performers the dancing diva Toni R. Andrews, the sexy Nilaya Milan Raven, and the creative whirlwind Kristi Waters. And then he paired these queens with celebrity queens from *Drag Race*, and hot damn, it made an amazing show.

When I started thinking about writing this book, Rey was the first person I wanted to talk with. I felt that in order to write a book with drag queens as a central focus I would have to do drag myself. I can't remember how I came to this crazy conclusion. Part of it was that I wanted to be credible as a writer talking about the concept of drag. And part of me was exhilarated by the thought that I could become something like the drag queen rock stars I saw on television! I could take creative and performance risks, all under the guise of doing research for the book, which gave me the cover to try something wacky and be able to justify it to other people. Did you see what I just wrote there? I felt I had to "justify it to other people." At this point in my life, I still cared too much about what other people thought.

I had heard of female drag queens but had never seen one in person. I didn't know what people in the drag business thought of them. Rey had allowed women into some of his amateur drag shows and was totally accepting of them. As Rey was my resident expert on drag, I implored him for help in how I might be able to do drag myself. He didn't hesitate. He picked up his cell phone and called Kelly Kline, his very good friend and the most revered drag performer in Austin, Texas. I had seen Kelly in person hosting the drag shows on Sunday nights at a local Austin gay nightclub, Oil Can Harry's. She had a commanding presence, and honestly, I was in awe and a bit afraid of her. If you were on your phone during a show or weren't paying attention, she would call you out from the stage, even playfully confronting you personally if she felt the need. And now Rey was asking her if she would help me learn drag.

"Kelly! It's Rey. Hey, I have this woman here, Jackie Huba. She needs a drag mother. Can you help her? She's in Austin." Kelly, now on speakerphone, instantly responded: "Yeah sure! Send her my way. Give her my phone number. No problem." Then he just hung up. Wait, what? What in the holy hell just happened? I have a *drag mother* now?!

A drag mother is often the person who first puts someone in drag. She is a mentor who teaches newbie queens the art of drag—theatrical makeup, wig styling, costume styling, the art of lip-syncing—and for male drag queens, how to *tuck*. I'll explain tucking, for the uninitiated. If you are a male drag queen creating the illusion of being a female, you have to learn to tuck or conceal your genitals by fastening them up and out of the way with adhesive tape. It's not an easy process, so I hear. So it's helpful to have a mentor teach you where to tuck them and how to tape them all in place. Luckily, I didn't have to learn how to do that. Now not all queens are lucky enough to have a drag mother. Knowing this, I nervously called Kelly to set a date to meet her.

I was not prepared for what I saw when Kelly arrived at my apartment a few weeks later. I knew she was a transgender woman, but I didn't realize how different she would be from the fierce drag entertainer I had seen on stage so many times. She was in her "day drag." An attractive curvy Latina in her early forties, she had her shoulder-length black hair pulled casually back into a ponytail. She wasn't wearing any makeup and was dressed in black casual pants and a short-sleeved, red Wonder Woman T-shirt. She was demure, reserved, and earnestly polite. This person seemed completely different from the sexy, assertive, outspoken, gregarious queen clad in Texas-sized wigs and long sequin gowns that I knew from the stage. The difference in the two Kellys illustrated to me how the creation of a persona through dress can completely change how people perceive you.

We talked about how she had first gotten into drag in Brownsville, Texas. Her friend's parents owned a gay club in town, and they used to let her in while she was still underage. She became enamored of the drag performers she saw there and decided she wanted to try drag herself. She entered an amateur drag talent competition and won. Then she entered the world of drag pageants, which are very similar to the beauty pageants that we have all seen on television. Drag performers are also judged on talent, swimsuit, evening gown, and a Q&A with the judges. Shortly after Kelly started doing drag, she won, in quick succession, Miss Brownsville Sweetheart, Miss Brownsville USofA,

Miss Rio Grande Valley USofA, and then went on to compete for Miss Texas USofA. Now, twenty years later, she has won too many pageant titles to list. As an experienced winner, she began to help other queens prepare for pageants, as well as mentoring new queens in the art form as their drag mother. These new queens are called her *drag daughters*, and Kelly has had over forty! Currently she hosts the top drag show in Austin every Sunday night, as well as other shows around central Texas five nights a week. Plus she has a day job as a makeup artist. She is one of the hardest-working people I know.

I was grateful and overwhelmed that Kelly volunteered to be my drag mother. I asked her what I should expect to learn. What she told me next has implications for all of us trying to create a fierce drag persona:

> You're Jackie right now. On stage, you're going to have to be a totally different person. Drag is about more makeup, more hair. Drag is over-the-top personality, performance, appearance, and confidence. It's a totally different level. You'll be wearing wigs. You'll be wearing as many bobby pins as we do. You're going to be wearing three or four pairs of eyelashes like we do. You're going to be contoured. Your boobies are going to be up to here. We're going to make you look like a totally different person. It's also nerve-racking as hell to perform as a character in front of so many people, because the moment you come out, you get judged by people no matter what. It's a "Well, let's see what you can do" kind of a thing.[3]

Kelly suggested we meet up at the local MAC Cosmetics store, which sells a staple brand of makeup for all kinds of theatrical performers, so she could advise on purchasing a starter kit of makeup. Kelly was like a kid in a candy store picking up foundation, concealer, eye shadows, eyebrow pencils, bronzer, blushes, eyeliner, lipsticks, lip pencils, mascara, and cosmetic brushes. In the coming weeks, Kelly spent hours at my house teaching me how to beat my face. Men who are trying to create the illusion of being female with makeup have to feminize a face with masculine features. Since I already have a feminine face, the idea was to use makeup to change my features to look like a different person. I still had to learn all of the makeup tricks that male drag queens use, including covering up one's eyebrows in order to paint on new ones. Kelly taught me how to contour, which involves using light and dark shades of makeup to sculpt the face into the proportions that are desired. I also mastered the art of applying and stacking false eyelashes because, honey, in drag, the bigger the better.

Wig styling is also a must. For my first performance, I learned how to pull my short brunette bob back, add on a black ponytail extension, and then spray the rest of my hair with black hairspray. It's that easy to change your hairstyle and color. Many queens will stack wigs in order to build volume. For my second performance, Kelly taught me how to layer two long brunette curly wigs on top of each other to create fullness. Then, for additional height, she took a short bob wig, turned it inside out so it became like a ball, and positioned it under the two other wigs to boost them higher. Some queens will put four or five wigs together for volume. There is literally no limit when it comes to how big one's hair can be.

As my drag character is inspired by Trinity from *The Matrix,* I decided that my costume aesthetic would be sexy, use the color black, and include boots. My first performance had a fetish theme. I shopped at Le Rouge Boutique, a store that calls itself "Austin's Emporium of Sexy" that sells sexy lingerie and novelties. I got a black bra with silver pointy studs on it, a black pleather cincher with silver flat studs, black fishnets, and a black high-waisted brief. I ordered thigh-high matte black boots from Amazon. And to top it off, I found a long, sleek black pleather jacket with small black sequins and black and teal feathers shooting out of the shoulders from the best costume store in Austin, and perhaps the country—Lucy in Disguise with Diamonds.

It took a lot of guts to go out and perform in this newfound getup. If it had been Halloween, when everyone is dressed up, and with a few cocktails, no problem! But for a woman in her late forties, with her ass hanging out a bit below a bodysuit, her boobs pushed up to the sky, and sporting thigh-boots, it was very daunting. However, the key to drag is to own how you look and not care what other people think. I don't have the body of a twenty-five-year-old. But I feel as sexy as I ever have in the long, luxurious brunette hair that I've always wanted. And so what if my ass is hanging out? Let this be a lesson to you! If I can go balls to the wall and become a female drag queen, you can take the first steps and make wardrobe and makeup changes in your life!

Not only was Kelly a drag mentor, she has also become a cherished part of my life. Though I am older than she is, to me she feels very much like a mother figure. She always had an encouraging word as I was learning these foreign makeup techniques. She listened to me go on and on about my insecurities in tackling drag as a woman and told me to just go out there and be fierce and own it. I was stunned when I saw a comment Kelly posted one day on a Facebook video that someone had captured of one of my performances: "[Lady Trinity] worked it out!! So proud of her!"[4] I instantly burst into tears. You see, I'd always longed for my parents to express pride in what I did. My parents are good people, but they've never been able to tell us children how they feel about us. Maybe it is their blue-collar background, or just their natural stoicism, but in all these years, I've never once heard "I love you," and certainly never "I'm proud of you." So when I saw Kelly's comment, it hit me like a ton of bricks. I didn't realize how much I had missed this type of parental love until I experienced it. This may be why I feel such affinity with my LGBT friends, who often have to create new families in their lives because their own biological families do not accept them. While not outcast by my family, I still am not close to them and have had to create my own family with my friends. In the drag world, drag daughters often take the last name of the drag mother, out of respect. Though I didn't take the last name Kline for my drag persona, I still feel part of the "Kline family" and treasure my relationships with Kelly and my fellow drag sisters.

 FROM THE STAGE

If Drag Can Make a Man Who Looks Like an NFL Lineman Look Fierce, What Excuse Do We Have? Meet Latrice Royale!

With a colossal wig and high heels, Latrice Royale towers over everyone at seven feet tall. She has a buxom frame and

Latrice Royale
(Photo by Marcelo Cantu)

confidently describes herself as "large and in charge, chunky yet funky."[5] Latrice's style is old-school drag pageant glam, with huge wigs and floor-length, shimmery sequin gowns. She may be a big girl but Latrice knows how to accentuate her swerves and curves. She uses corsets to cinch in her ample figure. At forty-two years old, Latrice (real name Timothy Wilcots) has been doing drag in southern Florida for over two decades. Latrice says drag saved her life. She is open about her eighteen-month prison stint for drug possession when she lost everything. After being released, she returned to drag, and it became her savior. She got back on her feet and made drag her full-time job. She competed in drag pageants but never won, most of the time coming in as first or second runner-up. She was looking for a national platform and auditioned for *RuPaul's Drag Race,* Season 4.

She made it on to the show and became an instant fan favorite known for her soulful lip-syncs and infectious laugh, like the Aretha Franklin of drag.

While some larger queens on the show used their size as an excuse for not looking good, Latrice never wavered in her self-confidence. "I have no time for insecurity. All the things I was insecure about I either had to love it or love it more. People prey on your insecurities, so why give people something to prey on? You can't be large and in charge and be insecure."[6] In fact, Latrice is not afraid to flaunt her gorgeous figure, even on the biggest of stages. In 2014, she was tapped to lip-sync Gloria Gaynor's hit song "I Will Survive" on a music and fashion showcase called "Fashion Rocks" broadcast on CBS. She started the performance in a floor-length black coat, which gave way to a skin-tight, gem-studded brown body suit that showed off her curvaceous figure. It was a glorious balance to the now slim and trim Jennifer Hudson, who joined Latrice onstage during the song.

Latrice lives every day by her mantra, "It's OK to make mistakes. It's OK to fall down. Get up, look sickening, and make them eat it!"[7] Translation: rise above your downfalls in life, and always look amazing while dismissing the haters. She explained to me in an interview, "I live by that because . . . people are going to be there trying to be negative or whatever, but the best form of revenge is success. If you can turn it around and take the power away from them, and make them eat every word they ever said, that's the ultimate. That's how I get my kicks when I get some of that, for real."[8]

So many of us have body issues, wishing we were thinner, taller, or just something we are not. Latrice is a shining example of loving who you are. And if all the trappings of drag can make Timothy Wilcots look and feel this good as a woman, then it can do the same for all of us.

 FROM EVERYDAY QUEENS

The MOB Wives of Richmond Are Magnificent, Outspoken, and Beautiful

"Everybody needs a queen in their life,"[9] or so says Anelica Mark-Harris, the de facto leader of the MOB Wives of Richmond. MOB stands for Magnificent, Outspoken, and Beautiful, which aptly describes this group of gregarious women from Richmond, Virginia. Ranging from ages fifteen

The MOB Wives of Richmond (*from left to right*) Arletha Phillips, Bessie Mark-Dillard, Anelica Mark-Harris
(*Photo by Sharon Poole*)

to sixty-one, these ladies have brought drag queens into their lives, and the association has transformed them. For forty-two-year-old married mother of five and small-business owner, Anelica, it all started with her fortieth birthday two years prior. She was going through a self-described midlife crisis and was not in the mood for a party. Her friends were pleading with her to do something big to celebrate this milestone birthday.

Before she knew it, her friends had taken over. Instead of the small get-together they had first described, they invited over a hundred people to her house, including six drag queens. Anelica, her mother Bessie, her aunts Arletha and Gloria, her teenage daughter Christina, and a few friends had been frequenting a local drag brunch for a while. Someone had invited these queens over to give Anelica a drag makeover for the party. Now sporting a blond curly wig, a fabulous over-the-top outfit, and big, blingy jewelry, Anelica was taken aback when she looked in the mirror: "It was just like an epiphany for me, where I just cried. 'Oh, my God I'm gorgeous.'"[10] It was a transformation that she didn't want to end. She wanted to experience dressing like a drag queen every day.

Anelica fully embraced the drag queen aesthetic from that day forward. She doesn't go out without a blonde lace front wig, of which she has many. When asked why the blonde hair, her response was straightforward: "Because I feel pretty in blonde hair. This is me. Why does black hair on a black girl have to be normal? . . . That's my thing, blonde hair is me. The makeup, the jewelry is me. This is just me, like I said."[11] She has custom-made dresses and outfits, each more sparkly and over-the-top than the next. She instructs the designer to add tags to the garments labeled size 0.

From then on, going to the drag brunch quickly became a monthly, then a bimonthly occurrence. Furthermore, everyone in Anelica's crew—her teenage daughter, her two aunts, and her mother—now dresses in drag queen couture. At the brunch, they started drawing attention among the audience of mostly straight women because of their looks, but also because they were the most raucous group there. Anelica told us: "This once a month [outing], all of us going to the club and just letting our hair down, is the coolest shit ever. This is our time just to be kids again. Our time to be college kids again. Just to get in a club, get silly for that two and a half hours and have fun."[12] The queens in the club jokingly began referring to the different groups of women using a "Housewives" designation, referring to *The Real Housewives of Orange County* reality television show and its spinoffs. One group was nicknamed the "Atlanta Housewives," another the "Beverly Hills Housewives." Vega Ova, one of the queens from the club, anointed Anelica's group the "Mob Wives," referencing a different housewife reality show series. Why the Mob Wives? "Because we were the loud, obnoxious wives," Anelica laughingly told us.[13] Her group got the joke, but decided to turn the word "Mob" into an acronym for Magnificent, Outspoken, and Beautiful.

It wasn't enough for the MOB Wives to just *look* like queens. They began *performing* as queens as well. Bessie Mark-Dillard (Anelica's mother and Christina's grandmother) decided a few years ago that she wanted her birthday party to be a giant drag show where she was the star. She transformed her large backyard into a club, complete with a stage, a sound system, a DJ, rows of seats, and a bar. Local queens lip-synced dance numbers until the star of the show,

Miss Bessie (her drag moniker), came out for her performance. The first two years Bessie performed Etta James songs. This past year, her sixty-first birthday, she lip-synced to Beyoncé. We watched the video of this party on Bessie's Facebook page. Miss Bessie emerged from behind a curtain made of shimmering gold foil tinsel, bedecked in a floor-length, body-hugging, strapless gold metallic gown, and proceeded to lip-sync *the house down*. We asked Bessie what part of performing in drag she enjoys the most. "All of it. Oh my God. The people, they love you so much. You cry when you are doing it. You actually feel like a movie star. It is not like karaoke, you actually feel like a star. You feel like that person that is singing. You become that person."[14]

Bessie and her sister Arletha are now performing in drag pageants in Virginia, sometimes competing with male drag queens. Arletha says: "[What] I love about competing is when I get dressed up, it's like a whole new ball game. I am the beautiful one in the room. Everybody's thinking that they are beautiful, but you'd be surprised when you've got somebody doing your makeup, you've got somebody doing your hair, fixing your clothes. When you look in the mirror, it's almost like Cinderella. You'd be like, 'Oh my God, look at this.'"[15]

Even Anelica's daughter Christina, now fifteen, loves drag queens. She started going to the drag shows when she was eight, first accompanying one of her aunts. She told us: "[The queens] have their dresses: they're big, beautiful, and [bejeweled]. They have the big hair. . . . When you look at them, it's like everything you want to be. They're so brave and they dress the way they dress. They don't care what people say."[16] Christina was so inspired by the confidence of the queens that she concocted an idea to wear a tutu to school every day in the sixth grade; this would be *her* drag. Anelica arranged for local drag queen Millenium Snow to come over every day before school and style a complete tutu-centered look for Christina, including makeup. Not many grade-school students have a stylist, let alone a drag queen stylist. Christina's looks were mostly a hit at school, but not with everyone. "A lot of people looked up to me. When I started wearing them, people started going, 'Why'd she start doing that?' There's always the [negative] people that [say], 'Why is she wearing all those clothes?' The drag queens built my confidence up. They don't care what people say. It built my confidence up a lot and it's like, well, I *want* to wear tutus at school."[17] So she did. Some people might be leery of letting their young children interact with drag queens. Christina has a message for them:

> I think it would help a lot of people to be exposed to drag queens. . . . I don't see anything wrong with that at all. . . . [Drag queens] have the mic and they'll tell you, "You can be whatever you want to be." And you have the confident [queens], the ones with the big hair. Like, they don't care, so why should you? I think this world would be much better if [more people] were exposed to more stuff like that.[18]

The MOB Wives, through their strength of personality, have built a worldwide following. At drag events around the world, you can't miss them with their signature chant, "Ain't no party like a MOB Wives party because a MOB Wives party don't stop. Toot toot. Beep beep." They began hosting their own MOB Wives–branded shows in Richmond, as well as crowning their favorite queens with the title of Miss MOB Wife. Queens as far away as Georgia, Florida, and Ohio have inquired how they can compete for this title. Anelica explains that they came up with the honorary title after one of their favorite local drag queens kept competing in pageants, pouring her heart into them, but never winning. They wanted the queen to know that she is always a winner in their minds. Now Anelica crowns whichever queen she deems the most deserving. She explains: "Drag is an art form and a community of people that are forgotten people. Once [the queens] have those three hours of fame on the stage, everyone wants to line up and take pictures of them, but what do they do when they go home? Who follows them? In our case, the MOB Wives of Richmond follows them."[19]

The MOB Wives are benefactors to the local drag queens in Richmond because they want to give back to the people who have so enriched their lives. Local queens are not like the celebrity *Drag Race* queens, who can often make drag their full-time job and tour the world. Doing drag is expensive, with all of the wigs, makeup, costuming, and so on, that it requires. Local queens often have full-time jobs and work hard for the modest fees clubs will pay along with tips from their audiences. Anelica advises everyone to go to his or her local club and befriend a drag queen. They'll appreciate the love, and you'll get a close-up education on how to be fierce!

The Psychology of Enclothed Cognition

What we wear is surprisingly complicated. Especially for women. Most men can get by relatively unscathed by choosing to wear either jeans or khakis with a decent shirt for work, downgrade that to a T-shirt and cargo shorts for the weekend, or upgrade to a suit, and they are golden. But women and their clothes are much more complex. We have learned through the media and decades of sometimes painful socialization that what we wear matters. Each occasion brings with it a host of expectations and concerns about what to put on our bodies. Does it look good? Is it (according to society) age appropriate? Will it attract just the right amount of positive attention without putting our safety at risk?—because we know that catcalls aren't just annoying, they are also associated with real danger. Can one move and walk in it, and does it even fit? It can be very tempting to ignore fashion and societal pressure and just wear whatever we want without worrying about all this—the world be damned! But I (Shelly) want to offer a word of caution. What you wear doesn't just send a message to the world; it also sends a message to your own brain. Because everything that you put on, that you enclothe yourself in, not only broadcasts outward who you want to be perceived as, it also broadcasts that same information inward to your own psyche. In other words, what you wear affects how well you think and how good you feel about yourself.

A research study at Northwestern University tested this very idea.[20] Their research led the team to coin the term "enclothed cognition" to describe the systematic influence that clothes have on their wearer's psychological processes, that is, on how their mind works depending on what they're physically wearing. Researchers gave two separate groups of people the same white coat. They told one group it was a lab coat for doctors and the other group it was a painter's coat for workers. Then they measured each group on how well they did on mental exercises that tested the subjects' ability either to pay attention to fine detail or to maintain sustained attention. The results varied according to two factors: the symbolic meaning of the coat and the physical experience of wearing the coat. In other words, if the subjects thought it was a doctor's lab coat and they also put it on, they tested much better. It's not just what's hanging in your closet, it's what you actually put on that matters.

So let's work our way around the wardrobe and the implications of the things we wear. For instance, shoes. To be precise, high heels. They make us feel more powerful, which makes us look more powerful. Timothy Judge, a professor of business at the University of Florida, examined the data differences in income for people who did the same jobs, focusing on the height of each person. He calculated that every inch in height corresponds to $789 extra in pay each year, even when gender, weight, and age are taken into account. He completed a meta-study of the research around this, including the implications of height for social esteem. The theory he examined implies that taller people are perceived by others as being more competent, and this carries with it greater expectations, which have a positive effect on self-esteem, which then motivates the person to perform better. Those who perform better earn more money. He also reports that the Bureau of Labor and Statistics confirms the monetary value height has for earnings. An extra six inches, for example, generally results in an extra $4,734 in annual income.[21] The taller you are, the more capable you appear and feel, and the more money you can earn.

Now let's talk about lingerie. Because, believe it or not, there have also been academic studies on our undies. Christina Tsaousi, in her doctoral dissertation for the University of Leicester in England, examined the choices women make when buying underwear and determined that, although in the past these purchases functioned only as supports for what went over them, it appears that our underwear serves as a method of changing the way women feel about themselves, their bodies, and their identities. We construct who we are as women by the choices we make in the lingerie department. How we clothe and care for our private parts informs our minds about how we understand our gender, and even our sexuality. Tsaousi discovered that women chose their underwear not only for its function but, more importantly, for the way they wanted to be perceived by the people who might see it. For example, if they knew that their athletic teammates or gym partners might see them in the locker room, they wanted to wear undies that were socially acceptable in that venue, which usually happened to be cotton and not visible in workout gear. If the women were visiting family members, or even in-laws, they wanted to make sure they packed "respectable" panties. But if they anticipated a possible sexual encounter, then they would choose to don the most seductive lingerie they owned. And in doing so, they informed others, and themselves, about their identity.

This study shows us that the way we care for ourselves by the panties we put on is also the way that we form our identity as sexual people.[22] It appears that our panties perform for us! So if you truly want to experience yourself as fabulous, then it's probably time to change your panties no matter what situation you are going to be in. White cotton probably isn't doing the trick, ladies! So the next time you're shopping for underwear, pick up some "power panties"!

Now on to the outfits you wear that anyone can see. How can you dress to be a more fierce, fabulous, powerful you? In the 1980s, women learned to wear power suits that were a reflection of the Iron Lady herself, Margaret Thatcher. As the first and only female prime minister of England, she was also the first modern political power dresser. She was famous for almost always wearing a blue skirt suit with big shoulder pads. For her, it was her armor. "I'm always safe in it," she said in a TV interview from 1984.[23] Her goal was to dress in a way that emphasized her ability to demand the same respect that men in suits garnered and at the same time maintain her own sense of femininity. Millions of women in business and politics adopted a version of Thatcher's power suit.

Since then, though, the female version of this eighties staple has morphed some to adapt to the particular field that businesswomen occupy. In 2013, Laura Abassi studied the clothing choices that female professors made on campus. She discovered that, although the dress norms for male professors have become much more casual, even without a written dress code the women still felt the need to dress in structured suits or dresses in order to gain control in their classrooms and avoid appearing overly sexual.[24] This confirms the Rule of Three T's that is currently making the rounds in women's business wear: No Tits, Toes, or Thighs.[25]

Women are painfully aware that introducing sexuality into the workplace can be a minefield. It's a bit different in the fashion industry, where the ability to artfully adapt the latest trend into something that looks both individualistic and beautiful is highly valued. In fashion, the business strictures for conformity are trumped by creativity and personal expression.

Whether it's a doctor's lab coat, a politician's power suit, a professor's respectable choice, or a fashion designer's creative ensemble, the clothes we wear have an influence on those around us and on our own self-image. The value in choosing something bold, risky, or fabulous is that we can experience what it is like to obtain more attention, and with it, perhaps more personal power.

 *notes* FOR YOUR DRAG DIARY

How to Look Sickening and More Tips on How to Dress for Power

Let's move on to help you determine what clothing makes you feel powerful. This *will* involve going outside your comfort zone or we're not doing our job! We've tapped Jackie's fabulous stylist Irene Scott, who has been helping women look their best for the past ten years, to help guide you on your way to dressing for power and confidence. You won't believe you've waited this long.

No More Oatmeal Dressing Pledge

"Oatmeal dressing," as Irene describes it, is a "kind of nondescript, non-exciting [way to dress]. It's kind of just

No More Oatmeal
Dressing Pledge

By signing this pledge, I AGREE TO
LOOK AS FABULOUS AS I CAN AT ALL TIMES.

....

I promise to put on something that I won't be ashamed of if a photo of it ends up on the front page of Buzzfeed.com.

I promise to wear jeans if I feel like wearing sweatpants.

I promise to wear one thing that makes me feel like Wonder Woman.

I promise to put lipstick on before leaving the house.

I promise to ask myself "what would a drag queen do?" if I am afraid to put something on.

....

Fiercely me, _____
[your name]

disappearing. It's comfort, but it's in a way that it's blah."[26] Sweatpants. Flip-flops. Baggy T-shirts. Oversize sweaters. These might be fine for cleaning out the garage, honey, but not for showcasing our most fabulous and confident self. We're not kidding. We want you take a "No More Oatmeal Dressing Pledge." Say the above pledge out loud. Or even better, go to EnterTheQueendom.com/pledge and print out the pledge. Fill in your name and post it in your closet. Take a picture of it and tweet it to @jackiehuba with the hashtag #NoMoreOatmeal.

Just a note here: sometimes we are dressing to impress others, and there is nothing wrong with that, if that is your intention. But what we are talking about in this chapter is dressing for ourselves. We are taking a lesson from drag queens (and psychology) that we can change the way we feel by how we dress. If we dress more fiercely, we can feel more fabulous and confident. You decide what you want to wear or don't want to wear, but know that if you want to feel bolder on the inside you must pay attention to what you wear on the outside.

Now that we've made the pledge of what we are *not* going to do, let's talk about how to dress to feel more powerful. Keep an open mind. Irene, our master stylist, shares her advice for taking fashion risks:

> Whatever your lifestyle or occupation is, it never hurts anything to put your toe in the water and try a little inner rock star, or inner drag queen. Give it a whirl. See what the feedback is. I've had a billion conversations where I'm talking people into things. I'm like, "Just try it. Just do it. Just wear it." Every single time, they're like, "Oh my god, I just loved it!" There should be always something where you go, "Well, I'm a little uncomfortable, but, god, that would be fun!"[27]

So let's have some fun! Experiment with the following ideas and record in your Drag Diary how each action you take makes you feel. Also note if the feeling of confidence you gained by changing your look helped you accomplish something you wouldn't have done before.

Start with One Bold Statement Piece

The easiest way to start, according to Irene, is to incorporate one thing into our wardrobe that is bold. Because we perceive it to be bold, just wearing it makes us feel bold. It could be a statement accessory, perhaps something in a bright color, or even a chunky necklace. Another idea is to create a power stack on your wrist with a wide-band metallic watch and a wide metallic cuff (three inches or more) of the same color. Remember those wide metal bracelets Wonder Woman wore that could deflect bullets? It's the same idea here. Or the bold statement piece could be your shoes. A bright-colored shoe looks good on everybody. Try a red one! It's not just for Dorothy in *The Wizard of Oz.*

Be a Minimalist

Irene advises having a punch list of basics that can be mixed and matched as your starting point. All women should have a well-fitted black suit or pencil skirt. A crisp white blouse. Dark dress pants in either black or navy. A dark pair of jeans. You want to have those basics that you could wear for ten years. Go and spend the money on some good-quality items. Then you can elevate the look and add power by adding the statement pieces we mentioned previously.

Even leather pants can be a staple, says Irene. "You should have a version of a rock star piece in your closet, even if it's just one thing. It could be a leather jacket. There should be something where you put it on and think 'I'm a little badass here.'"[28] Trust me on the leather pants. Irene talked me into them, and I love them. She's even talked her mother who is in her seventies into them, as well as some of her clients in their sixties.

Use Power Colors

Bright colors like red and orange bring out power. They are bold and draw attention. Black as a basis for your outfit is always powerful. Just make sure you aren't wearing *all* black—black shoes, black suit, etc.—or you'll just be the black version of oatmeal.

Red on the lips is also a power statement. Miss Fame, a megatalented makeup artist and supermodel drag queen, suggests that if you're a woman who's looking for the warrior within, get a red lipstick. She advises: "Honestly, a red lipstick, a matte red, or a shiny red lipstick will make you feel powerful, I swear. Find the right shade. Maybe it's an orange tone or a blue undertone. Those are colors that you can find depending on your skin color. . . . It showcases your mouth so your voice will be seen, because people will look. . . . You'll have to command that lip. A lot of people go, 'Oh, I can't rock that lip.' Yes, you can. Everybody can rock a red lip."[29] Russian Red and Lady Danger from MAC Cosmetics are two good red shades to try.

Step Up to Heels

Flats are for quitters. Now hang on, don't get too riled up. Yes, flats are comfortable and they are better for your feet and your posture. I (Jackie) went for comfort (or so I thought) over style by eschewing heels of any kind for most of my life. But since being transformed by the world of drag I now truly understand the power of heels. I often perform in high-heeled, thigh-high boots, so, honey, you know I've gotten over my indifference toward heels. The thing about heels is that they change our posture, our gait, our height, and they can also change how we feel. They can make us feel more powerful. If you're a heels gal then you already know this. If you're not convinced and don't normally wear heels, give it a try. Get it out of your mind that wearing heels equals searing pain in your feet. There are heels out there that are much more comfortable than others and also look good. For heels that you need to wear for more than a few hours, here are a few things to keep in mind:

1. Look for good-quality shoes, which will cost you a bit more, but it's better to invest in one good pair of expensive heels than three pairs of heels that kill your feet.

2. Stay under three inches as a rule.

3. Stay away from skinny stiletto heels, as they put too much weight on too little surface area, although Shelly swears by them.

And if all else fails, pick the most badass shoes you can find: any attention-grabbing low pump, a bright and shiny flat, or even a powerful purple combat boot!

If You're Not Wearing Nails, You're Not Doing Drag

This is actually the title of a song by one of my favorite drag queens, Alaska Thunderfuck 5000. Many drag queens love their long, adorned press-on nails. In the lyrics to the song, Alaska is jokingly making fun of lazy queens who don't bother to complete their female illusion by adding nails. Nails are a staple of the well-dressed queen. I never used to paint my nails until a few years ago when gel nail polish was introduced. Now you can walk out of the nail salon with completely dry, hard nails that won't chip and will last for about two weeks. This has changed my life! I am never without my nails done. I like to make my ring finger on both hands into an accent nail, either in a different, complementary color or by adding a thin layer of glitter polish on top of the main color. Having your nails done just completes your look. You look and feel put together and ready to tackle the world. It may be a small thing, but it can make your hands look as dressed up as you are.

Get a Stylist or Personal Shopper

It can be invaluable to find someone to help you develop that fierce style. A good stylist or personal shopper can bring together pieces that you would have never thought of before. If you're like me, who really needs the fashion expertise I don't have, they are a godsend. Lots of stores have free personal shoppers to help you. Of course, then everything you buy will be from that one store. But for big department stores or stores with a wide variety of items, this works well. Stores that have free personal shoppers include Anthropologie, Club Monaco, J. Crew, Macy's, Madewell, Topshop, and of course my go-to, Nordstrom.

If you want someone to come to your house and check out your clothes closet, then you are in the market for a personal stylist. They usually work by the hour or have set fees for specific services, such as auditing your current wardrobe, updating your wardrobe with select pieces, or creating a completely brand-new style. A great way to find a good stylist is to ask your well-dressed colleagues and friends for recommendations, or simply find one on the web through Google or Yelp.com.

For the Drag Curious

For our advanced readers, here are some ideas to really push your boundaries. You will be amazed at how liberated you feel once you try them.

- Go out on the town in a wig. You heard us, a wig. Find a wig that makes you feel like a completely different person. We could write an entire chapter on how to shop for a wig, so here are some quick tips. If you are looking to experiment with a wig and not pay a lot of money, check your local costume store. You can also find inexpensive wigs on Amazon.com with many under twenty dollars. If you want a wig that is more realistic looking and you have the funds to spend, shop where the drag queens shop, including websites such as RockStarWigs.com, WigsandGrace .com, or BobbiePinz.com. These higher-quality wigs can run from $40 to $150. Or try the Cadillac of wig sellers, WigsByVanity.com, with wigs priced from $100 to $250. Looking for wig-styling advice? Check out the thousands of YouTube tutorials. Once you have found your wig, it's time to go out on the town. If you are lacking courage, find a friend or two or six and make it a girls' night out, with all of you in your wigs. Of course, cocktails can be very helpful if you are feeling skittish about it. Here's the thing: you might look a little over-the-top, but who cares! Go to dinner and then head to a dance club in your city and dance the night away. You'll have a blast, trust and believe!

- Get a complete drag makeover. This one is a bit more difficult but completely worth it. The best person to do a drag makeover is a drag queen who is also a makeup artist by day. You might need to go to your local drag shows and chat up the queens. Find out if anyone does makeup for their day job and then hire them. They should also be equipped to style a wig for you. For your outfit, go to a local costume store, vintage store, or Goodwill. Find the most over-the-top outfit that your drag persona would wear.

- Go to your next costume party in drag. This is a no-brainer! It's a perfect opportunity to get yourself up in some drag. Everyone will be in costume, but *your* look is going to be sickening *the house-down boots!* Bonus points if your drag look makes you unrecognizable to your friends. In fact, make this your goal. Look as different as possible from your real self. As I pointed out in the last idea, you may need to hire a drag queen makeup artist for help with all this.

We'd love to see any or all of the things you've tried in this chapter. Make sure to take pictures and post them to social media tagging @jackiehuba with the hashtag #FiercelyYou.

Drag queens are masters at dressing for power. They command the attention of a room just with the over-the-top things they wear. All eyes are on them from the moment they step onto the stage. But it's also how they use their bodies *in* the costumes that creates power. When was the last time you spent money on an outfit that felt fabulous in the dressing room, but the minute you walked into an event you started to doubt yourself? Wouldn't you love to be able to keep that great feeling all the time? To know how to move your body in a way that feels good and reminds you of your worth, your power? Then let's sashay a few more steps farther into the Queendom!

The Third Key

❝ *When I'm feeling a little low, I put on my favorite high heels to stand a little taller."*

—Dolly Parton

Say the words "strike a pose" and the first thing that comes to mind is Madonna's 1990 number one dance hit "Vogue." What most people don't know is that Madonna borrowed (or stole, depending on your point of view) the idea of "voguing," a highly stylized house dance, from black drag queens in Harlem. In the nightclubs, the drag queens mimicked the rich, glamorous white women who strutted down Fifth Avenue and posed as models in magazines. They used intricate hand movements and exaggerated poses to tell stories of how they dressed in drag, applied makeup, put on stockings, and styled their hair. Full of these glamorous poses, the dance was called "vogue," after the well-known fashion magazine. Many dancing drag queens today use some form of voguing in their performances. The more current form of voguing involves spins, dips, duckwalks, and the *death drop*.

Whether they're voguing during a dance number or just standing in one place lip-syncing a dramatic ballad, drag queens radiate fierceness onstage by using powerful body positions that demand all eyes on them. From the moment a queen steps onstage she owns the place. Body positions and movements can increase feelings of power and confidence, and the rest of us can vogue in everyday ways by putting our bodies into higher power posture positions.

Are you ready to learn how changing your movements changes your ability to take risks? Are you ready to overcome your fear of owning your sexuality? Ready to use your body to become more confident in your everyday life? And to incorporate drag movements into your work, your social life, and even your exercise routine? Then let's do it!

Petrified in Pasties at Burlesque Class

When I (Jackie) first decided to do drag, I knew there would be a lot to learn. I don't have a background in acting, theater, or dance. I decided I would have to put myself through my own "drag boot camp." Drag queens are experts at seducing a crowd. This really scared me, because I've never considered myself a sexy person. As I've said, I was a computer science major and worked at IBM for over a decade, so I feel like I'm a bit of a dorky nerd. I'm goofy, not seductive. I've never really tapped into that sexy side of myself, and on the few occasions when I've tried to, I've felt like an idiot. Lady Trinity is supposed to be sexy and sensual, and so I thought the best way to learn how to express this was to do one of the scariest things I have ever done: take a six-week burlesque class.

I was incredibly apprehensive about going to the first class. I remember thinking when I got to the studio: "Are you insane? Why the hell would you sign up for a class where you have to strip down to pasties?" I was so nervous that I screwed up the time of the class and got there two hours early. The front-desk person at the dance studio suggested that I could fill the time at the restaurant next door and grab a drink. Yes! That was exactly what I needed—alcohol! Maybe it would help calm my nerves. Two glasses of red wine later I showed up back at the dance studio, ready to whip those clothes off! Well, not really.

Our instructor was a woman named Wendy Sanders, aka Ginger Snaps when she performs in burlesque. Wendy is a thirty-four-year-old vivacious, buxom redhead and immediately commands a room, whether her clothes are on or off. There were six women in the class, and Wendy suggested that we sit down on the floor, have everyone introduce themselves, and tell why we were taking the class. I could see that some in the group were already self-conscious. It was interesting to hear why these women were there. Most were in their thirties and mentioned wanting to tap into their sexiness for their boyfriends or husbands. One pretty petite young woman who looked to be around twenty-three—let's call her Lacey—excitedly explained: "I take other dance classes here, and I thought 'Ooh, burlesque seemed like it would be fun. So I thought I would take this!'" I envied Lacey her cheerful, nonchalant confidence in tackling this thing that I was actually petrified to try.

Then it was my turn to say why I was there, and I sheepishly explained, "Well, I'm studying to be a drag queen." I could see the looks on the others' faces, which was mostly "Um, what the what?" I explained I was writing a book on drag and felt that in order to write the book properly, I should do drag myself. Crickets. The silence added to my feelings of insecurity because I wasn't sure what they thought about my explanation.

Wendy had us stand up and start learning some basic burlesque poses and moves. They did not come naturally to me at all. One move was to stand with your back to the mirror, then turn and pose toward the mirror, all the while running your hands up your body, real sexy-like. We all tried this move, and I felt like a fool doing it. Meanwhile, Miss Lacey was next to me exclaiming in her girlish voice, "Oh, this is so fun!" With her flirtatious, ruby-red Mary Jane heels, short black pixie hair, porcelain skin, and red lips, she was gazing at herself in the mirror, pouring on the sex appeal, and looking just like a pinup model. I was now full-on jealous of Lacey, with shades of irritation. Every perky word she said was like nails on a blackboard. The more she exuded this unabashed sexuality, the more I felt inferior to her. This was exasperating, because I hate not being good at things. I hadn't come to terms with the fact that this isn't my strong point, so I was being hard on Lacey and extra hard on myself.

Playing the role of a sensual tease is miles away from anything I've ever experienced. I think perhaps it's because when I was growing up I saw my mother constantly push my dad's playful kisses and hugs away, which taught me to keep people at bay, especially men. So outwardly showing sensuality and vulnerability is very hard for me, a real struggle. (With that in mind, let's all take a moment of silence to acknowledge my poor, poor exes and the struggle it must have been for them too. Amen.) I managed to finish the class despite all of this, walked back to my car, and just sat there behind the wheel thinking, "How am I going to do five more weeks of this? It's only going to get worse." First, I couldn't believe I was arguing with myself about this in the car. And second, I was writing a book about fierce drag queens and self-confidence but was afraid of a little public sexiness? Oh hell, I was studying to be a *drag queen*. Well, then, what would a *drag queen* do right now? What Would a Drag Queen Do?

"What Would a Drag Queen Do?"

I thought about the advice I had gotten from Courtney Act, an international drag star, pop singer, and former *Australian Idol* semifinalist. She'd told me: "Whenever you've got a fear about something, it's not really real. It's your *perception* of how other people are going to react about how you think about yourself, in relation to the external world. Anytime that you have a fear, I think that is a sign for you to focus on it and understand why this fear of [yours] is something that is holding [you] back, because fears obviously hold you back. I think my advice for you [getting through the fear of something], is to do it and enjoy it. Why not?"[1]

So I took Courtney's advice and went back to that damn class. I made it through all the rest of the classes, but it wasn't easy. One of the hardest was learning how to twirl nipple tassels. I'll never forget when Wendy announced at the beginning of class, "OK, tops and bras off! Let's get those pasties on, ladies!" as she unceremoniously whipped off her shirt and bra. For the uninitiated, pasties are small cloth patches that are stuck on a person's breasts to cover the nipples and areolae. Long fringed tassels are attached to each pastie. As I mentioned earlier, Wendy is a full-figured beauty. When that bra came flying off, she was just standing there, exposed in all her glory, with boobs as big as your head. It was inspiring to see Wendy so fearless about her body. I thought to myself, "Oh my God, look at her, she's not insecure at all. She's living for it! Why can't I be this unselfconscious?" I wanted to be as strong and liberated as she was. So I did something I'd never done before: I commanded myself to take action in spite of my fears. And that's where I found liberation. I silently yelled at myself: "Fuck that shit. If she can do that, I can do this. So take off the bra, and stick on the pasties, Jackie!"

Slowly, five out of the six of us in the class did as we were told and removed our shirts (one gal left her bra on). Wendy lent us all multicolored sequined and/or beaded pasties with string tassels affixed and showed us how to use double-stick tape to stick them onto our own breasts. Apparently the nipple tassel twirl is not as easy as you might think. Getting those suckers to twirl involves trying different techniques: bouncing up and down on one's toes or doing the back-and-forth shoulder shimmy. There is something about standing there half-naked, boobs a-bouncing, watching the tassels go round and round in the mirror that brings on uncontrollable laughter. Try it for yourself and see what happens. You'll crack yourself up as much as we did.

Perhaps most daunting of all, each of us had to put together a striptease performance as graduation from our final class, including picking a burlesque stage name. Of course I used Lady Trinity. This burlesque performance was to be the first "outing" of a version of Lady Trinity, but luckily it would be performed only for the small audience of my instructor and five classmates. I choreographed a Marilyn Manson song titled "Ka-Boom Ka-Boom," complete with sexy poses, shimmies, and glove reveals that finally culminated in wearing vinyl boy shorts, fishnets, high-heeled boots, and nothing above the waist but the custom leather pasties I'd gotten from Etsy.com.

Performing for my class was one of the hardest things I'd done up to this point. Only three of the students including me even made it to the final class; maybe the rest were too scared to show up. One shy classmate performed her routine without ever removing a stitch of clothing. Who was the other student who made it to the final class? You guessed it: the personification of my insecurity, Miss Lacey, who, of course, killed it in her performance.

When it was my turn, I remember the music starting and just repeating to myself, "You can do this . . . you can do this." It was all a blur afterward, but I think I hit my choreography, and Wendy and my classmates were kind enough to whoop and holler during my performance. I had someone record a video of it, but to this day I can't bring myself to watch it. Yet I remember feeling victorious! If I could do a burlesque routine and strip down to pasties, then I could do anything! I felt much more comfortable and confident with my body after going through this experience. It really was a great preparation for forthcoming drag performances where my outfits would be a bit skimpy. What I learned is that the best way to get over something you are afraid of is to just try it.

Backup Dancers Make You Feel Like Beyoncé

Most queens in the clubs come out solo, lip-syncing a song. If they are comedic, they may use props. If they are good dancers, you may see a split or a death drop. Or they may be really good at interacting with a crowd. As a woman doing drag, I wanted to be more theatrical and more over-the-top than what I saw most of my local drag queens do. So I decided that I would always have backup dancers. I've never had formal dance training and just picked up choreographed dance moves from watching videos on MTV as a kid. I made it on to the drill team in high school—like the Rockettes but with pom-poms—and that was my last real dancing type of performance. Hello 1983! Drag queens who compete in pageants sometimes have elaborate dance numbers complete with backup dancers, so it's not unheard of in the world of drag. It's just not that common. Plus, if I'm going to be really honest here, at least I wouldn't be out there on the stage all by myself.

For my first set of performances, I was going to be a guest in the top drag show in Austin that is hosted by my drag mother, Kelly Kline. The show was at Oil Can Harry's, and I'd be performing with a cast of seasoned local queens. For the first show, I found a playwright/actor/director in Austin named Bastion Carboni to conceive and direct it. Bastion also dabbled in drag as his slutty, meth-thin, politically sardonic alter ego, Pilar Salt. I decided to use the song "Amazing" by the electro pop duo Hi Fashion. The song is a perfect anthem for knowing you are fantastic and not caring at all what others think of you. Here's a bit of the lyrics:

I don't care if you don't like my hair
Because I know it's amazing.
And I don't give a damn if you don't like my tan
Because I know it's amazing.
And I don't give two hoots if you don't like my boots
Because I know they're amazing.

And I don't give a shit if you don't like my tits
Because I know they're amazing.[2]

Bastion and I conceived the number with Lady Trinity playing a dominatrix-type role with her two backup dancers acting as her submissives. Besides dancing behind her, the dancers, at one point in the song, got down on all fours and formed a chair for her to sit and then lie on, while she continued lip-syncing. I have to say it felt really powerful to realize that these dancers were going to be my playthings. (On the stage only, people! Get your mind out of the gutter.) When we actually performed the number, I tried really hard to think of myself as this powerful bitch of a woman who was in complete control of herself, what was happening on stage, and two hot male dancers. What really helped me to inhabit this character were the wig and costume, very similar to what I had worn in my Lady Trinity photo shoot. By the time I got this whole getup on, I felt like the baddest bitch in the room. And the submissiveness of the dancers just fed into this feeling of being powerful. The key to the performance is radiating that power through your body at all times, whether you are moving or standing still. Shoulders back, tits out, fierce eyes and facial expressions. Drag is about standing in the limelight and completely owning your own power.

For my second performance on a different night, I wanted to push myself to do something even bigger. So instead of two backup dancers, I got four! My song selection was the dance hit "Smack You" by Kimberly Cole. While I can't identify with, or condone, the premise of the song, which is one woman wanting to fight another woman over a man, I did like the forcefulness of the lyrics, especially one line in the chorus, "Tonight I'm gonna smack a bitch." My friend Vu, who choreographs for his own flash mob group, put together a kickass dance routine, and I found two guys and two gals as backup dancers. It was a bit intimidating to be out in front of four really good dancers. I decided to let them do most of the hard moves and I would come in on the easier ones. For the costume, I got a brand new silver sequined body suit and studded cropped black jacket. I stacked two long brunette wigs with a third short wig curled up underneath for height. It somewhat resembled a 1960s-style bouffant look à la Jane Fonda in *Barbarella*. I felt so glamorous in the long sexy hair. When I took the stage with four backup dancers this time, I felt like Beyoncé! Now I certainly don't look or dance like Beyoncé, but I felt the power of having this supporting cast, whose sole mission was to make me look good. All eyes were on me! Ordinarily, so many of us women try our best to fit in, not stand out. But here in drag, it is all about standing out.

Crafting the mechanics of my drag performances taught me how important physicality is to feeling confident. I could have chosen any style of song to perform to, but I was drawn to heavy beat-driven dance songs. I liked the forcefulness of the strong dance moves, which fueled my feelings of power as I performed them. Thinking about how to express power with my body in drag performances has made me pay attention now to how I express power in my body in everyday situations: when I walk on stage to give my keynote speeches, when I walk into a conference room with my consulting clients, or when I attend a networking event where I don't know anyone—for all these types of situations I have learned that one of the best ways to look powerful and command attention is to make sure that one's body movements and posture express those goals.

Dragercising Will Help You Look Good and Feel Gorgeous

"Honey, know your words."[3] This was one of the first pieces of advice I got before I started doing drag. D. J. Pierce, better known as his drag alter ego, Shangela Laquifa Wadley, impressed this upon me in an interview the next day after he'd hosted the Austin, Texas, PRIDE Parade. "If you're performing . . . you want to connect with your audience who's watching you. You don't have to be a super experienced dancer, but if you're going to connect through lip-syncing, people connect through songs. If you don't know what you're saying, there's no way they can connect to you."[4]

I really took the advice seriously. I started listening to my performance songs all the time. I would lip-sync in the mirror when I was getting ready in the morning, but putting on makeup while moving your mouth is not the best idea. I found that one of the best times to practice my lip-syncing was when I was walking my dog.

There was a park across the street from my condo building near downtown Austin called Sand Beach Park. The park was a giant rectangle with a concrete sidewalk bordering all sides, around one-third of a mile long. This was my usual route to walk Béla, my small white toy poodle. With earbuds in my ears and my sunglasses on, I would blast my performance song on my iPhone while walking the dog around the square loop over and over again. But I didn't just nonchalantly mouth the words to myself; I lip-synced the shit out of that song! Not a sound was coming from my mouth (or at least I couldn't hear it), but I was acting out the lyrics with facial expressions, hand gestures, and body language. I was strutting to the beat like I was on a runway in heels. This helped me practice expressing power through my body as I took every step.

I'm sure I was a spectacle to other joggers and dog walkers as I was *feeling the fantasy*, walking around the park over and over, and gesticulating to music that no one else could hear. At first the looks I got made me self-conscious, but after a few more walks I didn't care! I was living for my lip-sync walking, or "dragercising" as I began calling it. I started doing this a few times a week. I found songs other than my performance songs that were fun to dragercise to. One of my favorites is "Looking Good and Feeling Gorgeous" by RuPaul. Who knew there was a way to get your fitness time in and practice your lip-syncing skills and power moves all at the same time? Plus you get to hone your "I don't give a crap what people think of me" skills as well. I can't wait for you to try it and report back! Go to EntertheQueendom.com/dragercising for a playlist of songs to dragercise to.

 **FROM THE STAGE**

Jujubee Has Two Left Feet but Can Still Own a Room

Boston-based drag queen Jujubee doesn't dance or sing live, but she *slays the children* with her fierce lip-syncs. Thirty-one-year-old Jujubee (real name Airline Inthyrath) studied acting in college and uses those theatrical skills to channel the emotions of the songs in her performances. Jujubee was second runner-up on Season 2 of *RuPaul's Drag Race* due in

Jujubee
(Photo by Nick Lovell)

large part to her magnetic personality. She is the most followed drag celebrity from the show on Facebook, with over five hundred thousand followers. In 2010, she was nominated for a NewNowNext Award for "Most Addictive Reality Star."

While other drag queens are jumping into splits or death dropping the house down, Jujubee channels all of her energy and power into her lip-sync instead of moving all around the stage. She shows that there are different ways to channel power through the body. Whether it's a ballad or an upbeat pop number, Jujubee uses her facial expressions and the lines of her body to act out the song. It takes an innate fierceness to entertain audiences while not using up much of the stage. Jujubee explained to me, "I can't dance and I'll never claim that I can. I won't lie to you, but performance for me is just evoking an emotion. I don't care if it's good or bad. I want to tell a story, and that's the kind of music that I love. . . . Say if you listen to a Jennifer Hudson song or a Whitney Houston song, you know when this song is about love, that she is in love and she wants to tell this man or this person that she wants him, now. Or if there's a song where somebody's really upset, I want to convey that story as well."[5]

I'm not a dancer, but I'm not *not* a dancer! I can identify with Jujubee and asked her advice on how to connect with an audience. She advised: "The most important thing about drag performance is to just go out and perform for the audience, because the audience is there to see you. They've paid money, but they also want to see that you're having fun and that you know what you're doing on the stage. You could just stand there and perform, and if it's telling a story and it's exuding that love for the art, they're going to love it. Then there are the [queens] that go out and just dance and do kick splits and stuff but there's a disconnect. You almost feel as though they're just going through [the motions], and it's beautiful movement, but you don't feel it sometimes. So, balance that."[6] She also gave me advice on owning my power on stage, which is also relevant on this stage we call life. "You may not feel as confident inside, but if you're exuding that confidence, people are going to [get] that from you. . . . They're going to see that if [you] can go over that rock or whatever is stopping [you], [they] can do it, too. I think that's inspiring."[7]

No matter what situation you're in, people are connecting with you, reading you, reading your body language and facial expressions. It doesn't matter where you are or what you're doing, whether you are in a boardroom, on a sales call, or negotiating while buying a car, you can project power by using physicality just like Jujubee does. She has a quieter power than her dancing-and-death-dropping drag sisters, but she shows us that you don't have to be gregarious and perform with over-the-top antics to command attention.

 *notes* FROM EVERYDAY QUEENS

How Brendan Jordan Posed His Way to Viral Success

"Day one coming out of my mom's womb, I was already showing attitude," says Brendan Jordan, the Las Vegas teenager who became a viral sensation in 2014.[8] In October of that year, Brendan stole the spotlight from a reporter who

Brendan Jordan
(Photo by Brendan Jordan)

was broadcasting live at the celebration for a new mall opening in his hometown. He just happened to be standing behind the reporter but in front of a huge crowd when "Applause" by Lady Gaga began playing on the loudspeakers for the party. Gaga is his favorite artist, so he began to mimic the choreography from the video—posing, turning, and giving fierce looks right into the camera. Using his sheer diva presence, he grabbed viewers' attention and made it impossible to concentrate on what the reporter was saying. A video of the news segment was posted on YouTube, and overnight it went viral, thrusting the fifteen-year-old into the social media spotlight. Media outlets around the world, including *The Today Show*, MTV.com, the *Huffington Post*, CBC.com (Canada), and the *Mirror Online* (UK), were infatuated with the "diva kid" who video-bombed the reporter with his dance moves and attitude. The media attention led to an appearance on the Queen Latifah show, with Brendan doing his signature diva poses. RuPaul was such a fan of the teen that he sent a drag queen to the show to invite Brendan to the finale taping of the next season of *Drag Race*.

Capitalizing on all of this attention, Brendan started a YouTube channel on which he discussed fun topics ranging from his favorite fashions and his eyebrow makeover tutorial to serious topics such as his coming-out story. As of this writing, Brendan has 553,000 followers on Instagram and 243,000 subscribers to his YouTube channel. His videos have been viewed over ten million times. Retailer American Apparel tapped Brendan for an advertising campaign after seeing the teen wearing outfits on Instagram created by mixing items from both its men's and women's lines. He has even walked the runway in a fashion show for celebrity fashion designer Marco Marco, known for his outrageous, glamorous, and over-the-top costumes for Katy Perry, Nicki Minaj, and Britney Spears.

In mid-2015, Brendan declared that he was gender-fluid after first coming out as gay the year before. Gender-fluid people do not feel confined by the restrictive boundaries of stereotypical expectations of women and men. In other words, a gender-fluid person may feel more female on some days and more male on others, or possibly feel that neither term describes him or her accurately. Hearing of Brendan's public coming out as gender-fluid, pop star Miley Cyrus subsequently invited him to be part of a photo shoot for her Happy Hippie Foundation, a nonprofit whose mission is to rally young people to fight the injustices facing homeless youth, LGBTQ youth, and other vulnerable populations. Miley and her foundation partnered with Instagram for a campaign, titled #InstaPride, to bring visibility to the lives and stories of transgender and gender nonconforming individuals. Brendan, his sister Hailey, and mom Tracy all participated with Miley in a photo shoot for the campaign with other LGBT youth that was covered extensively by *Time* magazine and other mainstream news outlets. Brendan was excited to be part of the campaign because he wants to be a role model for LGBT teens and inspire them to be out, proud, and confident of who they are.

When I asked Brendan where he got his confident attitude from, he said it might have been from one particular family member: his great-grandmother Maci. "I think my great-grandmother is a very big inspiration because she's so sassy. She's eighty-five, and she tells me the stories how other men would whistle at her. She'd tell everyone she's not married when she really was, just to make herself look younger, and how she'd always go out in five-inch heels to the grocery store."[9] Brendan also loves drag and is inspired by the drag performers he has met. "Drag queens have opened my eyes to a whole other world. . . . [They] have probably inspired me to be confident because I see other people doing what they see [themselves] as and that makes me want to do it. I'm not only copying them but I'm just making it my own."[10] He says the sassy, confident Brendan character we see in the videos is him, but amped up a bit for his online audience. "I classify myself as a shy person. Believe it or not. I really do. . . . I think Brendan is a character. I think Brendan is a drag queen if that makes sense . . . the makeup and sassy outfits, that's all part of the Brendan character."[11]

In fact, I first met Brendan in person in May 2015 in Los Angeles at RuPaul's DragCon, the first drag queen convention in *her*story. As a YouTube star, Brendan was invited to appear and be part of a session where he would be put into drag for the very first time. Phi Phi O'Hara did Brendan's drag makeup and styled his Lady Gaga ARTPOP-inspired wig before an excited crowd of fans in a breakout room at the convention. When I asked Brendan about the experience of being in drag for the first time, he told me, "You honestly feel the change. You feel like your soul has left your body. It's really like you're a new person. . . . You just got charged. Batteries are put into you or something. It's weird." He says that in drag, "there's no flaws about you, and you know that. . . . I feel like an angel, if that makes sense. I feel like [I have] no insecurities at all."[12]

All you have to do is look at the comments on Brendan's social media to see how much he has inspired people of all ages. Even LGBT people in their twenties and thirties tell Brendan they wish that they had had this much confidence to be out and proud at such a young age. Unfortunately, one cannot have as many YouTube views as Brendan has and not get haters making vile comments on his videos. Not only does he get homophobic insults lobbed at him on social media, he also has received criticism, surprisingly from gay men, for being so openly flamboyant. Brendan is as deft as a drag queen in deflecting all of this negativity. "I can't spend my whole day thinking about what one person said to me," he told me. "If a person hates me, then, 'Oh, well.' . . . My strong support system is the reason why I do not give up. I know myself to not let that one thing get [me] down. I know where I'm going. I know my future. That person might be a little pebble or rock in my future, but I'm stepping over it. I know where I'm going. . . . That's why I'm not letting it get to me."[13]

Make no mistake; Brendan is more than just the latest viral sensation. He is committed to using his fame to advocate for the LGBT community. Pride Toronto, one of the largest annual Pride celebrations in the world with 1.2 million attendees, selected Brendan as their first ever Youth Ambassador in June 2015. He's participated in LGBT anti-bullying and anti-smoking campaigns, and filmed coming-out videos with other LGBT YouTube stars. Brendan believes we should always showcase our inner fabulousness to the world. "I feel like that's what God makes us. I feel like He makes us all drag queens. We just get out of costume sometimes."[14]

All of these amazing things have happened to Brendan because he wasn't afraid to be himself behind that reporter at the mall. He wasn't afraid to showcase his signature diva poses when his favorite Gaga music came on the loudspeaker. To borrow a phrase from Anelica of the MOB Wives, Brendan was born "genetically fabulous" and he knows it. But here's the amazing truth: So. Were. We. Who knows what wonderful things might happen to us if we dare to showcase *our* fabulousness to the world?

 FROM THE COUCH

The Psychology of Nonverbal Behaviors and Their Effects on Hormone Levels and Risk Tolerance

It is absolutely stunning how changes in dress, movement, and posture can affect how we experience ourselves. Science tells us that nonverbal behaviors have a much larger impact on our lives than most of us imagine, especially when it comes to self-confidence and a personal sense of power. When researchers examined people who demonstrated power in their relationships with others—that is, determined who was the "alpha"—they noticed some striking similarities. The indicators of power, or being in charge, according to Thomas Shubert and Steffen Giessner of the Netherlands, are a steady gaze, an expanded posture, and greater height and/or size relative to the people around one. Specifically, whichever person is taller, larger, or simply occupies the physically higher space in a room will possess the hormonal surge that accompanies these actions. The first indicator, the steady gaze, was researched by Yale professor John Dovidio and his colleague Steve Ellyson.[15] They measured the amount of eye contact that a speaker and listener maintained and discovered that the person who was perceived as more powerful was the one who held eye contact while she or he was speaking, and *not* while she or he was listening. This implies that if you want to assume power, the first thing to do is hold eye contact with others while you talk or perform.

Expansive posture, the second indicator, happens to be a popular topic these days in the plague that is commonly called "manspreading." If you haven't seen images of average-sized men, legs wide apart and taking up two seats on the subway, I encourage you to look this up online. Women do this in a different way, usually by parking their purse or tote bag on the seat next to them. The reason we tend to have a somewhat negative gut reaction to this behavior is because it is a not-so-subtle display of power. Organizational behavior professors Larissa Tiedens and Alison Fragale examined subjects who were seated opposite an unknown collaborator who changed posture from a constrictive, arms-and-legs-tucked-in-close position, to a more expansive, arms-and-legs-spread-wide position. Even though the subjects would try to match whatever position they were presented with in order to feel more comfortable, they were mostly maneuvered into adopting the opposite posture. All subjects reported feeling more powerful when they were spread out and less powerful when they were tucked in tight.[16] In addition to self-perception and feelings of power, scientists have also measured the change in testosterone levels of people who change their posture. In fact, doing two one-minute expansive poses is enough to boost testosterone to a level that can cause people to feel more powerful.[17] What this tells us is that if you find yourself feeling less powerful than you wish, try taking up more space than you normally would. Spread your arms out to the side and see what happens!

The third indicator of power, height and size, is pretty straightforward, with an added twist. It's not just larger and taller people who command more power; it's also being *perceived* as higher or bigger that makes a difference. Researchers Serena Chen, Annette Lee-Chai, and John Bargh studied the effects of sitting at a desk in a large chair versus sitting at the desk in a small chair. As you would expect, whoever sat in the big chair felt more powerful and was perceived as more powerful, regardless of their actual size. The opposite held true, too. Those who sat in the smaller chair felt inferior, even if they were actually larger than the person in the big chair.[18]

These posture changes affect us in such a powerful way due in large part to the neurotransmitters in our brains and the hormones in our bodies—specifically, dopamine, serotonin, oxytocin, and testosterone. It's biological. Confidence, it turns out, is created and sustained by more than one of our genes, these hormones, and the combination of how we think and what we do. Our thoughts, actions, and biology all play parts in how we perceive ourselves as powerful and confident; so this means that how we use our bodies can cause changes in our brain, and those changes can help us feel more powerful. It's a wonderful cycle.

Dopamine is the brain messenger that gets us moving. It is the substance associated with curiosity and risk taking. Without it we become bored, passive, and depressed; too much of it and our brains become swamped and unable to think clearly. The two genetic variants of dopamine clearance in the brain will move us either toward adventure or toward fear and fighting. For the purposes of this book, we're looking at the person who perhaps tends to worry about making the right choices. They may sometimes overthink things or get stage fright and freeze up under stress. As you think about taking the risks this book recommends, this could be you. However, taking risks can actually help you process stress by removing the built-up dopamine so you can keep moving and avoid giving in to a flight, fight, or freeze response.

Then there's serotonin, which works in our prefrontal cortex, the part of our brain that makes thoughtful, rational decisions. Serotonin also quiets the amygdala, the more primitive, reactive part of our brain that, if left unchecked, can cause us to fight, flee, or freeze during stress, and eventually leads to depression. When we find ourselves under duress—for example, in a roomful of scowling people who are waiting for us to speak—we might shift into a freeze mode because the memory of a similar time in third grade when the class laughed at us is readily available to our brains. But if we have an adequate supply of serotonin in our systems, then our brains can shift to the upper lobes and access rational thought. The memories of successful events are stored there. So the more successful events we create for ourselves, the more serotonin we have stored. When we are successful at taking risks, it helps our brains as well.

Oxytocin, another neurotransmitter, floods our system with hope and happiness. It's called the "love hormone," because scientists have examined the brains of people who are in the throes of a new love relationship and found that they are awash in oxytocin. People who tend to have a high level are more optimistic, more resilient under duress, and are able to access their prefrontal lobes faster than those who are low in oxytocin. The good news is that oxytocin isn't just for lovers—any positive social experience can increase it. That's why a person who can walk into a room and smile at folks will feel all warm and fuzzy inside when the smile is returned.[19] And that's another reason why it's important to push ourselves to take risks and find new positive social experiences to build up our cache.

What you should take from this section is that stepping up, striking a pose, and shining those pearly whites can bring about positive changes in your brain, which will mean more powerful brain chemicals lined up to support you!

 FOR YOUR DRAG DIARY

Feeling the Fantasy in the Boardroom and the Living Room

Now let's look at how you can create confidence by manifesting the fabulous person in your head and moving her into reality or, in drag slang, "feeling the fantasy." Are you ready to let the world see your power? Here's the thing, though: by exhibiting power using your body you are going to draw attention to yourself. This attention is what gives you power. You have to get comfortable with standing out, knowing that it is for the right reasons. You aren't always going to feel confident in every situation, but you need to will your mind to make your body take power positions anyway. You learned earlier that just by putting your body in these positions you *will* feel more powerful.

You may feel that some of these ideas are silly or wacky. That's the point! The idea is to take action—*to do something*—that forces you to try new things and learn from them. Some of these ideas will test you, will force you not to care what other people think. You'll be surprised. Many people are going to say, "You go on with your bad self!"

Dragercising

We've already talked about the concept of dragercising. Now it's time to try it. Put a few songs on your phone or iPod that are upbeat and you know the words to. (Don't forget you can always use our playlist at EntertheQueendom.com /dragercising.) Put on your workout gear, bring your earbuds, and make your way to a place that is good for walking. With your earbuds in, turn the music on, begin walking, and start your lip-syncing! Use your facial expressions, your hands, and your body to act out the song as you walk with the beat (get dance songs for some good cardio!). If you see someone looking at you, just smile and keep on going. Sunglasses really help here, because you can pretend you aren't seeing people. You'll be surprised at how amazing you feel as the energy of the songs propels you onward. You're belting out the songs but you aren't making a sound! Record in your Drag Diary how the dragercising went—how you felt when you first started, while you were doing it, and after you finished.

Walk the Runway

Where others might see a hallway, grocery store aisle, or mall concourse, drag queens see a runway. It's a place to showcase your fabulousness just like a supermodel. This activity involves walking in an ostentatious yet casual manner, typically with exaggerated movements of the hips and shoulders, otherwise known in the drag world as sashaying. Drag star Miss Fame explained to me how she thinks about the way she carries herself in public: "When I walk, I walk with purpose. In my head I imagine that there is fire burning behind me, or the ground is breaking beneath my feet. Even in high school I did that. Something in my head said I was meant to be seen and I was supposed to do it that way, visually. It's about imagining yourself in this greatness and giving yourself this sense of ownership that you're worth it."[20]

Find your runway. Any longish space with a clear pathway will work. Now, with shoulders back and chest out, stare directly ahead. Put a defiant look on your face that says, "You wish you were as fabulous as I am!" Now put one foot in front of the other and walk with long strides. Imagine that you are walking on a rope by keeping one foot in front of the other, which will allow your hips to swing from side to side in that classic model way. Wearing heels will make you feel even more powerful. If you are in a place where you can play some dance music and walk to the beat, even better. Walk to the end of your runway with your gaze locked straight ahead. When you get to the end of the runway, stop and cock your hips to one side, and place one hand (or both) on your hip(s). Give an acknowledging look to your invisible admirers on either side of the runway. Turn with flair and walk back down the runway toward where you started. If you are doing this in public with other people around, again, dark sunglasses can help. They make you feel mysterious and cool and give you a sense of anonymity. If you are taking part in the **50 Days to Fierce Challenge**, have a friend record a video of your fierce runway walk. Then post it to Twitter or Instagram, tagging @jackiehuba with #FiercelyYou.

Womanspreading

"Manspreading" made it into the *Oxford English Dictionary* in the year 2015. As Shelly mentioned earlier in this chapter, the term refers to men on public transportation who splay their legs wide apart and encroach on neighboring seats, to the dismay of women everywhere. Whatever motivates the men who do it, it's a dominant power move. It says: "I own this space. You find another place to sit."

Expanding our posture is a power move everyone can use, not just men. In the "Notes from the Couch" section, we talked about how placing the body into positions of expanded posture changes our physiology and makes us feel more powerful. It also can send a message to those around us that we are the power player in a room. Try one of these power poses the next time you are in a room at work or in your personal life in a situation where you want to assert your power.

- Stand with your hands on your hips like Wonder Woman.

- Stand in front of a table, lean forward, out-stretch your arms so they are straight, with just your fingertips touching the table. This works especially well if you are leading a meeting and you've lost control of the discussion.

- Sit back in your chair, lean backward, place the palms of your hands behind your neck, and interlock your fingers.

Make Yourself Bigger

This concept is similar to womanspreading, but instead of using expanded body positions, we use everything else we can to make our presence bigger. Just as in drag, bigger is better when it comes to most things. Here are some things for you to try:

- Bring more stuff. Are you in a conference room at work where you need to show confidence and power? Get to the meeting early, sit near the middle of the table, and take up as much space as you need for your paraphernalia (laptop, notebook, phone, etc.). Taking up space at the table commands attention.

- Wear heels. Being taller expands your appearance. At those times when you need to be powerful, more height is helpful. Take a lesson from the professional women in New York City who carry their heels with them on their commute and change into them before they walk into the office.

- Stand up straight and tall. This works especially well in a meeting if it's done with finesse. If you are seeking to command attention, find a way to get into a standing position. Perhaps go to the whiteboard and diagram the concept you are proposing. Suddenly all eyes will be on you and you'll become the most powerful person in the room. Use that power wisely, though; refrain from monopolizing the meeting.

In your Drag Diary, write down the strategies that worked best for you and think of new situations where these power moves might also be successful.

For the Drag Curious

For our advanced readers, here are some adventurous ideas that really make a fierce statement. To be sure, they involve more costuming, but if you can find a way to try them, you could incorporate a version of them into your everyday life.

- Wear bigger hair. Bigger hair makes you look bigger. It adds to your presence. It could be just wearing your hair long, in waves or curls, or teasing your hair for more volume. Or it could be—our favorite—adding a wig. Now you may not do this at work, or maybe you will! But perhaps first just wear a wig to a normal (read: not costume) party and see how you feel. You will get attention, but it will also make you feel powerful. Don't forget to post your big-hair photos to social media, tagging @jackiehuba with #FiercelyYou.

- Make an entrance. Enter a room with confidence and capture people's attention. Perhaps no one enters a room like a drag queen more than Taraji P. Henson's Cookie Lyon character on the hit television show *Empire*. Cookie is a "whole lotta sass" and a "whole lotta ass," and she's not afraid to use both of them to steal a scene. She's a master at knowing how to make an entrance. She often makes her presence larger by wearing huge fur coats and flashy animal-print outfits. Google "Enter Cookie: An Empire Supercut" to watch a video montage of her best entrances from Season 1 of the show.[21] Now perhaps you don't need to be as flamboyant as Cookie when entering a room, but here are some general tips:

(a) Take your time and don't rush into a room. Pause outside the room if you need to gather your thoughts and composure.

(b) Make sure you have a strong posture. As you enter, walk with confidence but not arrogance. Keep your head up, your shoulders back and down, and smile.

(c) Stake out a position on the other side of the room and stride confidently toward it, not hesitating or getting sidetracked. Motion captures attention.

(d) Make direct eye contact with those you want to stop and speak with.

Using power moves to project confidence and steal the attention is a drag queen's superpower. But all that attention tends to draw criticism too. Another drag queen superpower is the ability to ward off all criticism as if wearing an invisible shield. Going outside your own comfort zone, and doing things that surprise your social network will also draw criticism. So how do you deal with that? How do you shake off those comments? And, more important, how do you get that inner critic, the one with the most power to scare you, to shut the hell up? Well, aspiring queens, we are here to help.

The Fourth Key

TELL YOUR CRITICS TO SASHAY AWAY

> **"**I don't care what you think about
> me. I don't think about you at all."
>
> —Coco Chanel

Although drag queens are celebrated for their performance art, they are also magnets for criticism. Anyone who is flouting gender norms seems to ruffle feathers in our still heteronormative culture. Also, though there are no rules in drag, as many of the drag queens I (Jackie) interviewed for this book proudly told me, that's never stopped one queen from giving her opinion on another queen's makeup, wigs, costume, dancing, and so on. All of this criticism has bred a kind of tough-as-nails culture in the drag world. Successful queens learn to shake off the haters and not worry about what other people think. Over the years, drag queens have also developed a set of "give as good as you get" rituals known as *reading* and *throwing shade*. Reading is when you incisively expose a person's flaws, often exaggerating or elaborating on them. Throwing shade is when you assume a superior attitude and subtly criticize, demean, or insult. In the words of drag queen Dorian Corey from the seminal 1990 documentary on drag-ball culture, *Paris Is Burning*: "Shade is, I don't have to tell you you're ugly, because you know you're ugly."[1] Shade is often so subtle that one sometimes doesn't realize one was insulted until later. To show the difference, a read would be "Your dress is ugly"—direct and to the point. Reads can be long or short. If someone were to say in a very condescending tone of voice, "Oh honey, I'm so glad you saved up to buy that dress," that's shade. You and your dress weren't insulted directly; the insult is implied by the voice and the context of what was said. You know it's ugly.

You don't have to be Hillary Clinton to know what it's like to receive as much criticism as drag queens. For female celebrities and politicians, commentary on everything from clothing to hair to bodies to personality is fair game for the media. In the workplace, the same is true. Research conducted by Kiernan Snyder, a linguist and tech entrepreneur, that looked at performance reviews for high-tech companies showed that 59 percent of the reviews received by men contained critical feedback, whereas 88 percent of the reviews received by women did. In the critical reviews of men, 2 percent mentioned negative personality feedback. For the women, it was 76 percent.[2] That's quite a disparity. Actually, it's shocking.

Not only do you have to deal with external critics, you also have to deal with your own inner critic. That's the voice that tells you that you aren't good enough, smart enough, or skinny enough. It's the negative self-talk that can prevent you from taking risks or trying new things. Women often have louder inner critics than men because we have been socialized not to stand out, so when we seek to do so, our inner voice challenges us. You need to find a way to neutralize the criticism coming from inside in order to move forward and grow. So let's look at how these queens have taken on their inner and outer critics and told them to sashay away!

Lady Trinity's Disquieted Debut

"But I'm not ready!" I told my drag mother Kelly Kline.
After I'd spent four months learning theatrical makeup,
practicing with my backup dancers, and lip-syncing in front
of my mirror, Kelly pressed me to set a date for my first
performance. "You're never going to feel totally ready," she
told me. "You just have to get out there." I was going to have
to *actually* perform in drag and stop procrastinating. It
seemed like forever ago that I had come up with this wacky
idea to actually do drag myself as research for this book.
Finally we set a date in December to perform in her weekly
drag show at Oil Can Harry's. Cue the panic. My inner critic
went into overdrive. "What if the audience doesn't like you
because you are a woman? What if they think you aren't
'draggy' enough? What if you forget the choreography and
freeze on the stage? What if you forget some of the lyrics?"
To make matters worse, I had invited all of my friends,
many of whom had never been to a gay bar or seen a drag
show before. No pressure!

It was the night of my debut performance and I was
backstage with my backup dancers, Cameron and Bastion.
Luckily I had convinced Kelly to put us on second in the
lineup so I could get the damn thing over with quickly. I
didn't want to be hanging out backstage for very long
because I knew my anxiety would grow with every passing
minute. I had triumphed over my fear of doing a full-out
burlesque performance in front of my class of five people,
but this was a whole new ball game. Now I would have to
perform in front of more than a hundred and fifty people
alongside seasoned local queens. The stakes had gotten

much higher. I was trying to channel the courage I'd gained after stripping down in burlesque class to this new challenge, but my uneasiness was reaching new heights. Bastion could sense it. We were minutes from going on, and he brought my face a few inches from his own, pressed both sides with his hands, looked straight into my eyes, and said, calmly but forcefully: "You got this. We've practiced and practiced. You got it down cold. Now go kill it."

We heard Kelly introduce me. There was applause and cheering as the music started. Then it was just sheer panic for the first ten seconds. Instead of entering from the back of the stage (which is really just the dance floor in the club), I thought it would be cool to emerge from the front of the stage, passing through the crowd. What I didn't anticipate was that the club had put a VIP table right in the place where I wanted to enter the dance floor and since the club was packed with rows twenty people deep around all the sides of the dance floor, we couldn't see the table from the back of the crowd. My dancers went ahead of me and parted the crowd, but they couldn't get through when they got to the table. Meanwhile, because I couldn't figure out what was holding them up, I began flat out *pushing* them forward, screaming "Go!" But they couldn't. The lyrics were starting and I wasn't even on the dance floor. "Shit! The whole thing is ruined!" I remember thinking. It had seemed like an eternity before we were able to literally fight our way through the crowd, but in actuality I only missed about ten seconds of the lip sync.

I turned to the crowd, assumed a power stance, and began to lip-sync mid-lyric. Like a quarterback who had just thrown a horrible incomplete pass in the end zone, I had to shake off the entrance, turn it the hell out, and throw a touchdown pass. It was just sheer willpower that made me move forward and get the performance going. Everything was a blur after that. I remember collecting some tips from people, mostly my friends. The song ended. People were cheering. We left the stage. Oh my god. What just happened out there?

Later I watched the video footage of me performing, and you know what? I didn't totally suck! In fact, I uploaded it onto YouTube, tweeted it to a few of the drag queens I had interviewed, and many of them said that they wished they had looked that good at their first performance. Wow. That really made me feel good. I am proud that I—literally—pushed through the adversity and kept going. I almost succumbed to my inner critic but was able finally to shut her up. My ability to tackle new and bigger things outside my comfort zone was steadily growing. I was slowly building a reserve of confidence that I could tap into to try new and bigger things. When my inner critic started injecting doubt into my mind, I remembered how I had already conquered some pretty big fears; and you know what, I survived. Not just that, I kicked ass! And so can you. But you have to push yourself to try new things in order to feel that rush of achievement and channel that feeling later.

 FROM THE STAGE

Love Her or Hate Her, Trixie Mattel Is a Standout

When Brian Firkus performs in drag as Trixie Mattel, it's impossible to look away. Trixie looks like a mutant platinum-blond Barbie with huge exaggerated proportions,

Trixie Mattel
(Photo by José Guzmán Colón)

clad in a range of pink hues and wearing giant white pumps. The makeup is jarring, to say the least. Brian explains the origins of Trixie's look: "I was looking at vintage dolls from the seventies and began painting my face the way they were drawn. The more Trixie embraced comedy, the more I wanted her to be a fifty-fifty split between a clown and a living doll. If you're supposed to paint for the back row in drag, I like to think that I paint for the Denny's down the street. The cheeks are strong because I want you to know that I am a man. I want you to be like, 'This idiot has paint on his face.'"[3]

The inspiration for his drag character came from dark times in his childhood growing up in a small town in Wisconsin (Silver Cliff, population 529). "When I was younger, I had an abusive stepfather. He would call me a

Trixie when I was acting too feminine or gay or being emotional," explained Brian.[4] He took the name Trixie, a slur his stepfather derisively called him, and turned it into something to celebrate in drag. By doing so he took the derogatory voice of his loudest critic and turned it around into something positive. That is one surefire way to gain confidence! Trixie's last name is Mattel from the company that makes Barbie dolls. As a young boy, Brian had wanted to play with Barbies and other girls' toys but couldn't because of his stepfather. He decided that if he couldn't play with dolls as a child, he could become one in drag.

To say that Brian stands out from other queens when he performs in clubs around the world is an understatement. A skilled makeup artist and trained actor, comedian, and singer, Brian told me: "Nineteen out of twenty drag queens are going to put on a pretty wig, a pretty jumpsuit, and do a popular song. That's not the type of drag that leaves a mark either. I picked up on that early on. I knew I was too weird to get booked, but I never saw it as a bad thing."[5] In the early days in Milwaukee he did have a hard time getting booked in local gay clubs because of his out-of-this-world look. But he stayed true to his artistic vision. Brian says that there is an advantage to not conforming to what is expected: "The presence my look commands is huge, because the look is unlike anybody else. Because it's so far away from a face you would see anywhere else, even if you hate it, you can't really look away from it, and that's where a lot of the power comes from."[6]

Brian's strategy of standing out worked. The one and only RuPaul took notice and selected him to compete on Season 7 of *RuPaul's Drag Race* after his first audition. His look was instantly polarizing. *Drag Race* had never cast a queen like Trixie before, and the worldwide fan base was vocal on social media, either loving or hating his Barbie-on-steroids look. But his quirky sense of humor made him a fan favorite, and he finished in a respectable sixth place despite being eliminated early and brought back again (long story). The show has given Trixie a worldwide fan base, and she now travels the world, delighting fans with her offbeat performances.

If Brian had listened to the cynics early in his career who cautioned him to tone it down and look more human, he would not be having the mountain of success he is having today. I asked him his advice for anyone who is dealing with criticism and doubting him- or herself:

> You have to be in love with what you're doing. When you are in love with what you're doing, you don't give a fuck what other people are saying, you really don't. That sounds so cliché, I just don't care.
>
> I tweeted a couple of weeks ago, "If you're not feeling my look, I'm feeling it enough for everyone, to be honest." I fucking love the way I look in drag. Even though it is weird, that's exactly what I like it to look like. If you don't like it, that is so not important, compared to how much I love it.[7]

I've heard this advice from more than one drag queen: you have to be in love with all that you are presenting to the world. Because if you truly are, no one else's opinion will matter to you. The key here is that you need to give yourself permission to be who you truly want to be. Once you start listening to critics and conforming your look, your personality, or who your friends are, you lose your sense of self. You become merely who others want you to be. It's easy to become insecure when this happens and succumb to negativity. Don't let that happen. Be like Trixie and love yourself enough for everyone.

 FROM EVERYDAY QUEENS

No One Can Drag Down London's Fierce Female Queens

Can women do drag? This question generates an enormous amount of discussion—potentially divisive discussion. It's true that, for our culture, the practice of drag has long been embraced and claimed by the gay community. It's been a way for the men who were ostracized, bullied, and attacked for expressing themselves in ways that the dominant culture labeled effeminate to parody that and take it to the extreme. These men were so good at dressing as women that they frequently fooled the straight community, and it was (and is) a delightful way to say "Fuck you!" to the haters. In fact, part of the appeal of drag is the unexpected paradox—the eyes say, "What a sexy woman," while the brain says, "Wait—that's a man!" And then the audience members who don't feel threatened by the conundrum or their own latent homosexual stirrings are able to laugh and enjoy the performance and to appreciate the artistry involved in this transformation.

But what happens when women decide to do drag? Suddenly, the tacitly agreed-upon structure has shifted, and some people, especially those who consider themselves purists, get offended. London, England, has a burgeoning scene of female drag queens, and they have dealt with this type of criticism before. One of London's female drag queens, Victoria Sin, explains, "The worst misogyny that I've encountered has been in gay spaces, basically looking me in the eye and telling me, 'I hate you because you're a woman and this is not your space and you don't belong here.'"[8] Lolo Brow, an award-winning neo-burlesque and female drag performer in London, has felt the sting of criticism as well: "I have had [audience members] on stage find out I'm a woman half way through. They refuse to listen to anything I say after that."[9] Holestar, a female drag pioneer in London with an eleven-year career, has dealt with the "vile misogyny" of some "bad" queens. "Women doing drag is still not mainstream," she says. "Recently I got called a cunt and 'some chick who thinks she's a drag queen' by a queen who I called out for plagiarism. Who the fuck says drag is owned by men? It never has been. It was carved out that way through pantomime and tradition, but if you look at old music halls you'd have lots of gender performance by both men and women."[10]

The London female drag queens aren't afraid to claim this space loud and proud as "drag feminists" (our term, not theirs). There doesn't seem to be as much discrimination in Austin, Texas, as the queens in London have experienced, but the struggle is real. Their ability to shake off the criticism and claim the art form as their own is impressive. Instead of letting the misogyny and hateful comments wear them down, they've formed a community of female queens who encourage each other to keep performing the art they love. They don't stand alone; they have the support of each other. Lolo Brow notes how this performance art form is changing with the times: "Drag isn't necessarily a man dressing as a woman anymore. It's become an art form. It's become a culture. Women have a place in that as much as anything." Eppie, a newer female drag queen on the scene, says: "People might assume that I'm a guy just because I'm dressed like a drag queen. I don't mind that, because I don't think my gender should matter. It's not like we have to ask permission to do anything, we just go ahead and do it."[11]

You don't need to ask for permission. This is the lesson to be learned from female London queens as they fight to make inroads into yet another male-dominated profession. How ironic is it that the profession is all about dressing up as a woman?

 FROM THE COUCH

The Psychology of Internalization and Rumination

Why are we so hard on ourselves? Almost every client who comes to see me (Shelly) has at some point realized that he/she is his/her own worst critic. I find myself saying time and again, "I bet that critical voice that sounds like you started out as someone else's voice. Let's figure out whose it might be." Because that is how internalization works. We take those early, constant criticisms that we received in life and begin to tell ourselves the same damned things. And, over time, we start to believe that those statements about us, which might just have been the insecure projections of other people, are true. It becomes an internal dialogue that keeps us from shining the way we are meant to.

Negative internalization usually starts when we are very young, and for women especially, it starts with the way that girls have been socialized to "be nice." We've been taught this since we entered pre–Mean Girl stage (around third grade) and realized that popularity matters. One way to stay in the popular group is to try and be extra nice and sweet to everyone. In her book *Queen Bees and Wannabes,* parenting educator Rosalind Wiseman calls that tactic "Going for the Miss Congeniality Award." Her seminal book changed the way in which adults view girls' friendships and conflicts, showed the way they interact in cliques, and suggested ways in which parents could help girls navigate those minefields. It even became the basis for the movie *Mean Girls.* In the book, Wiseman writes that, unfortunately, this is how girls are trained to internalize negativity:

- When you're with your friends, always put yourself down, especially in comparison with them, and compliment them. (When you're not with them, you can say what you think.) Picture what happens when one girl tells another girl how great she looks. Does the recipient of the compliment thank her? Rarely. Instead, the response is usually some variation of "Oh no, I look so fat and horrible. I can't believe you would say that. You look so much better than me." Girls must degrade themselves after being complimented in order not to appear vain.

- Leap to your friends' defense when they put themselves down; they'll leap to yours when you put yourself down. So you say you're fat? "OMG, you look so good!" Girls literally competed with each other about who's the fattest. ("You're so much thinner than me, compared to you I'm such a cow.")

- And don't do any of the above too much because then it will look like you're begging for compliments all the time, and that's annoying.[12]

Not only have we been taught to be nice, put ourselves down all the time, and compliment others at our expense, this kind of criticism (both from others and from ourselves) takes a toll on our very health. Daniel Goleman, Harvard-educated psychologist, author, and current director of the Consortium for Research on Emotional Intelligence in Organizations at Rutgers University, has written over twenty books about social and emotional intelligence that address the impact of human interactions. In his book *Social Intelligence: The New Science of Human Relationships,* he writes about the sensation of "hurt feelings" and how our brains register social rejection in the exact same part (the anterior cingulated cortex) that is known to generate the sensations of bodily pain.[13] Furthermore, he states that

being evaluated threatens our "social self," the way we see ourselves through others' eyes. Our self-worth comes from all the messages we get from others about how they perceive us. And a threat to our standing in the eyes of others is almost as powerful to our survival as a physical threat. If we receive a hostile reaction that triggers our fears of rejection, our bodies produce some of the highest levels of the stress hormone, cortisol, than any other factor that has been tested. And this is just as true *if the judgment exists only in our imaginations!* Because the moment that you think it, you create an internal representation, which then acts on the brain exactly the same as it would in real life.[14]

To make matters worse, internalization is often accompanied by rumination. Rumination is the "compulsively focused attention on the symptoms of distress and on its causes and consequences, rather than on its solutions."[15] Rumination tends to sound like this in our minds: "Oh no! I really screwed that up and now they all think I'm stupid. This always happens, and now I feel like crap. My stomach hurts. Oh, god, my heart is racing. What's my pulse? Is it high? And now I'm starting to cry. I always cry. What a baby! My nose is running and my face is turning puffy and ugly. Now my head hurts so bad. Oh, no!" This negative feedback loop in our minds can completely derail us from finding a solution to the problem that triggered it in the first place. Even worse, the rumination loop can actually cause us to become ill.[16]

It is so important to find ways to end that internal dialogue that keeps us from being our best selves. So when we find ways to combat it, as the next section shows us, we are able to rise above it!

notes FOR YOUR DRAG DIARY

How to Tell Your Critics
to Sashay Away

This is where you put that knowledge to work for yourself. For your Drag Diary homework, you are going to work on how to curb the inner critic and dismiss the external dissenters.

Take a Self-Talk Inventory

Get out your Drag Diary. Open to a clean page, where you are going to keep track of the things you say to yourself for a week. Date the top of the page and draw a line splitting the page in half. Label one column "Critiques" and one column "Affirmations." For the next seven days:

- Put a tick mark in the "Critiques" column every time you find that you are thinking something negative about yourself, along with a word or phrase that you used. If you use that word/ phrase again later, add a new tick mark beside it. Otherwise add the new word/phrase to the column.

- Put a tick mark in the "Affirmations" column every time you encourage yourself or say something positive to yourself with a word or phrase that you used. If you use that word/phrase again later, add a new tick mark beside it. Otherwise add the new word/phrase to the column.

At the end of the week, make a list of the top five self-criticisms and the top five self-affirmations. Don't be discouraged if your "Affirmations" column is a lot shorter than your "Critiques" column. It just means you've started the process of self-improvement. Congratulations!

Now, above the list of those top five self-criticisms, write in all caps FELICIA.

Your Inner Critic's Name Is Felicia: Tell Her Bye

Yeah, that's right. We just gave your inner critic a name. And we think her name is Felicia. Most of you know what happens next: we get to tell her, "Bye Felicia." For the uninitiated, "Bye Felicia" is a line from the 1995 comedy *Friday*, in which actor/rapper Ice Cube coolly dismisses an unpleasant mooch named Felicia. The catchphrase is now used in pop culture as the ultimate kiss-off or dismissal of someone or something one finds irrelevant or stupid. For each of your self-criticisms, you are going to imagine that it was this bothersome person Felicia who uttered it. You are going to create a response to each particular criticism and *read Felicia to filth*. In fact, you are going to imagine if you were a drag queen how you would respond to Felicia's critique. Legendary drag queen and LGBT activist Sylvia Rivera once said, "Hell hath no fury like a drag queen scorned."[17] Well, you are a queen and your negative self-talk, aka Miss Felicia, just pissed you off with her nasty comments. Time to put that bitch in her place!

Now let's look at those top five self-critiques from the previous step that nasty Felicia has voiced. For example, let's say Felicia's criticism is about you being too fat. Now we ask ourselves, WWDQD? Or "What Would a Drag Queen Do?" with this comment? Your response might be: "So what if I'm fat? Is skinny a requirement for being fabulous? Must not be, because FAB-U-LOUS is what I am. Bye Felicia!" Do this for each of Felicia's criticisms. Write them down in your Drag Diary. And even better, say the responses out loud to a mirror with all the verve and sass you can muster!

Your External Critics Are Also Named Felicia

Yes, it's true! This idea of taking a criticism and responding with a positive comeback works for both our internal Felicia and our external Felicia. That dude in your department at work who is always criticizing you in front of the team is a Felicia as well. So when you're on the receiving end of a derogatory comment from someone, don't let it get you down. Before you grow angry or start obsessing about the comment, just stop. Remember, it's only Felicia spouting off her negativity again. Just as you did with your internal Felicia, write down the person's comment in your Drag Diary followed by your witty retort with a "Bye Felicia" at the end of it.

WWDQD? Reminders

Write WWDQD? on your bathroom mirror in red lipstick. Put it on a 3″ × 5″ card and tack it up on your bulletin board at work. If you are looking for something a little more fancy, head over to EnterTheQueendom.com/WWDQD for free printable templates and other fun items you can use.

Rumination Stopper

As you learned earlier, rumination is when you compulsively focus attention on something that went wrong and why and how it shouldn't have happened rather than accepting it and moving forward. It's like a downward spiral of emotions that makes you just want to sit on your couch and eat an entire pint of Ben & Jerry's Chunky Monkey in your pajamas all day while watching *Golden Girls* reruns. Not good! If you find yourself starting to ruminate on something, here's a surefire way to stop it:

1. Acknowledge the situation. The first step to solving the rumination spiral is to admit that it is happening. You are spending way too much time on it and it isn't helpful.

2. List three things that went well that week. To break the negative cycle of rumination, think of three things you accomplished in the last week that you are proud of. This will help reroute your thinking toward positivity.

3. Get moving. Exercise will help you get the body moving forward, and the mind will follow. Dragercising, anyone?

Dealing with criticism is never easy, especially when some of it is coming from inside one's own head. There are no better role models than drag queens from whom to learn how to shake off skeptics. When you stop yourself from internalizing negativity and ruminating about it, you free yourself to try new things outside your comfort zone. You will be ready to take risks like a drag queen. Can you imagine the things you could accomplish if you learned how to relish the risk?

The Fifth Key

> **"** *When I wake up in the morning, I feel like any other insecure twenty-four-year-old girl. Then I say, 'Bitch, you're Lady Gaga, you better fucking get up and walk the walk today.'* **"**
>
> —Lady Gaga, June 2010[1]

Lady Gaga understands that in order to overcome our insecurities and lack of confidence, we have to work through our fears while taking action anyway. So does RuPaul. His biggest hit song, the 1993 dance hit "Supermodel (You Better Work)," says it perfectly. (We changed the spelling of "work" in our fifth key for extra fierceness!) Just *thinking* you are fabulous and fierce like a drag queen or a super-model is a start. But in order to be really confident, that fierceness needs to propel you to take action. Real confidence comes when you take that action even though you are afraid of possible risks.

Drag queens are some of the most hardworking people in show business, and they are constantly striving to keep their performances fresh. This means taking risks by trying new looks, new songs, or new dance moves every week. There's little time to perfect these, so queens have to exude confidence when bringing new routines to the stage or else the audience can see the doubts. There is no time to ruminate

133

over what didn't work in the last performance. Cynthia Lee Fontaine, a Puerto Rico–born but Austin, Texas–based queen who has won many drag pageants, told me: "There's no comfort zone for drag. The moment that you feel the most scared is that moment that you have to execute [your] plan. Because that's the . . . best way that you can figure it out."[2]

Lip-Syncing for My Life alongside Drag Superstars

"I AM EXCITED TO TELL YOU THAT YOU ARE INVITED TO PERFORM AT OUR FIRST ANNUAL AUSTIN INTERNATIONAL DRAG FESTIVAL!!!"

This was the opening to the e-mail that I (Jackie) received from Jamie Steward Bancroft, the organizer of the first ever Austin International Drag Festival, one of the biggest drag events in the world. This brand-new three-day drag festival in May 2015 in Austin, Texas, would include over two hundred performers from more than ten countries performing in venues around the city. Every type of drag performer would be featured at the festival, including bio-queens and drag kings. Headliners for the event included legends of drag such as Lady Bunny and Jackie Beat. Also performing were stars from *RuPaul's Drag Race*—Adore Delano, Courtney Act, Jiggly Caliente, and Pandora Boxx—as well as Derrick Barry, the top Britney Spears impersonator in the world. Podcasters and YouTube stars focused on drag would be recording shows at the event. The event was so packed full of all things drag that some dubbed it the "SXSW of Drag" after Austin's huge annual music, film, and web festival, SXSW. And I—well, Lady Trinity actually—had just gotten accepted to perform.

When I first heard that the festival was taking applications for performers, I was intrigued. I thought about applying, but then my inner critic started talking some smack. Most of the performers coming to the event had years and years of experience doing drag, and for the celebrity queens, it was their full-time job. I had only performed in drag twice before this. Who was I, this newbie queen, to perform alongside them? I didn't want to embarrass myself. But on the other hand how could I pass up applying? One of the biggest drag events in the whole world was going to take place in my backyard. Was I really going to be too *afraid* to be part of it? I began to confront my inner critic: "What's the worst that could happen? You probably won't get selected anyway. You don't have enough experience. But you'll never know unless you try. So just fill out the freaking application already!" I finally completed the application, and a month later I was in!

At first, I felt ecstatic. I was beyond grateful and excited that someone as new to drag as myself would get the opportunity to perform along with such talented and legendary artists. Just when I'd conquered something big in this drag journey, I found myself taking on something even bigger. I kept pushing myself to take on new challenges and learn as much as possible. I wanted to take this drag experience as far as I could, because I could feel myself growing in confidence in everyday life, and I loved that. But that doesn't mean the nerves weren't there. Performing at the Austin International Drag Festival was not like performing in a local club. This would be doing drag before a much bigger audience (several hundred people) in a show full of the top drag performers in the world, which was damned intimidating. But I was determined not to let that fear stop me. How else would I learn and grow?

I had to get to work. Each entertainer had to perform two numbers. I decided to do my "Amazing" number and a new one set to "Vanity" by Christina Aguilera. I had to find new dancers. I had a new costume made that was a takeoff on a fierce red bodysuit that Jennifer Lopez once wore. I paired that with some kick-ass shiny red vinyl thigh-high boots, and bam! It looked hot, if I do say so myself.

Before I knew it, it was the weekend of the festival. Friday and Saturday were spent watching other queens perform in music venues around Austin. I was in awe of the legendary comedy queens Sherry Vine and Miss Coco Peru, who have been making audiences laugh for the last twenty-five years. Then Sunday night came and I was ready. My first performance was the "Amazing" number I had done before. Same costume, same choreography, swapped out one dancer for another but no biggie. Since we knew the routine already, I was confident it would go well. And it did. The lip sync was on point. We nailed the choreography. We got lots of tips from the crowd. We killed it! I was so proud of the performance.

The second performance, though, was a different story. I had decided on the "Vanity" number at the last minute, which only left time for two practices with my four dancers. I was feeling really nervous about the number, but I hoped that having that many dancers up there with me might lessen the risk and ease my worries. Safety in numbers, right?

Wrong. First, I had to follow Derrick Barry, the world-famous Britney Spears impersonator. Derrick has been performing for over ten years as Britney and most recently was doing his act five nights a week at the longest-running celebrity female impersonator revue in Vegas, called Divas Las Vegas. To say that Derrick is a professional entertainer doesn't begin to describe him. He did two twenty-minute performances, dancing and lip-syncing to all of Britney's hit songs. His makeup, wigs, and costumes are identical to those of Britney, and to be honest, with his sexy, skimpy costumes showing a lot of body, he looks as good she does. How was I supposed to follow that? I had interviewed Derrick for this book a year earlier, so I knew him a little. He told me that he would make sure to come out of the dressing room to watch me perform. I wanted to die.

It was time for us to go on. I stood at the bottom of a short set of steps leading up to the stage in the dark lighting of this cavernous music venue. We waited to be introduced. I thought about Derrick somewhere in the dark in the back of the club, watching me. Panic set in. "I can't do this," I said to myself. I could feel the sweat on my palms. I was afraid I was going to look like a neophyte or stupid compared to all of the seasoned queens who performed on the stage that night. As the music started, my heart went into overdrive. My dancers moved up the stairs onto the stage, but my feet felt like they were glued to the floor. I couldn't move. I was a queen in the spotlight but I felt like a deer in the headlights. I was frozen in fear. What in holy hell do I do now? From nowhere, an inner voice commanded: "You get up on the stage, Jackie. You get up there RIGHT NOW. You cannot turn back. You are going to get up there and FUCKING DO THIS!"

And so I did. I triumphantly stepped up onto the stage and . . . tripped over my own two feet, lunging forward a bit. Ugh! This started a chain reaction of being off the mark of my carefully choreographed moves. I kept going, but as I moved to the front of the stage I tripped again. Then, as I tried to get out of my long outer coat, it got stuck on my arms and wouldn't come completely off. I had to hurry, pull it off jerkily, and just throw it in the general direction of one of my dancers, who was supposed to be helping me get it off. What in the hell was happening? I felt completely thrown off balance. The next thing I knew, as I was still trying to keep the routine going, I turned and ran smack into one of my backup dancers. So, yeah, it was going as horribly as I could have imagined. For a split second I thought, "This is so terrible. I want to quit and just walk off the stage *right now*." I was embarrassed and humiliated. But as I looked out into the crowd, I saw that most people in the audience were smiling back at me. I saw that some people had their hands outstretched with dollar bills in them. They were tipping me! (Good drag audiences know to tip their drag queens.) And in that moment, I thought to myself, "What Would a Drag Queen Do?"

"What Would a Drag Queen Do?"

Would she leave the stage and disappoint her audience? No! She would put a smile on her face, keep going, and finish the song. So that's what I did.

I finished the number and got offstage as fast as I could. I wanted to run and hide somewhere in the dark corners of the club and not see or talk to anyone. But I decided to buck up and make my way back to the dressing room. On my way there, I ran into another drag performer from the show who, apparently, had just watched my disaster of a number. To my surprise, she came over to me, gave me a huge hug, and said, "Girl . . . you were fabulous!" Whether she really meant it or was just trying to make me feel better, I have no idea. Then it hit me: she was right! I *was* fabulous. I'd just done something that I was absolutely terrified to do. I put myself out there to get into this festival and I performed as a drag queen, with other queens I respected. Who cares if it didn't come out perfect? Or even if it was pretty bad? So what? The important thing was that I had gone outside my comfort zone and tried something that scared me. If I could do that, I could do anything.

Still, I had to stop myself from ruminating about what I could have done differently. My inner critic started in on me, "If only we'd had more practices it would have been better." "Stop!" I told my inner Felicia. I took a risk and accomplished something that most people wouldn't even have tried, and I should be proud of that. And I was. And at least I looked good! I will always have this experience of having worked through my fears to accomplish something I was petrified to do. I can draw on that success to give me strength and courage whenever I'm afraid to do something. And the next time I need to muster some confidence I will think, not "What Would a Drag Queen Do?" but instead, "What Would Lady Trinity Do?"

"What Would Lady Trinity Do?"

She would lip-sync for her life. There is nothing she can't do!

Derrick Barry on the Merits of "Just Showing Up"

One drag performer who knows the power of taking risks and trying new things is the same Derrick Barry that I mentioned earlier. Derrick first grabbed the media spotlight when he performed as Britney Spears on NBC's reality competition show *America's Got Talent* in 2008 at age twenty-four. When I interviewed him for this book in 2013, he shared with me one of the most important pieces of

Derrick Barry
(Photo by Christopher DeVargus)

advice he ever received. It was from Mariah Carey's former tour manager, Christine, who was also a producer on *America's Got Talent*.

> I said to Christine, "I can't believe the opportunities I've had because of *America's Got Talent*. Thank you." She said, "You need to thank yourself, because you showed up. The rest just happened. You showed up." I love that, because now anytime I'm thinking, "Should I do it, or should I not?" All I've got to do is show up. The rest is going to happen. It's beyond my control, but if I don't show up then I'm never going to know. Then I'll never be considered for it and then . . . why wonder what if? When all you have to do is put yourself out there.[3]

Just. Show. Up. Three simple words that make so much sense.

Derrick has been showing up for new adventures his whole life. He began training as a gymnast at the age of five. Seven years later he moved from gymnastics to theater, starring in over twenty productions between junior high and college. At nineteen, he moved to Hollywood to pursue his dream of being an actor. On a whim, he dressed up as Britney Spears for Halloween in 2003 and saw how much attention he was getting as he walked down Santa Monica Boulevard. He told me: "I got an amazing reaction right away. We were walking . . . and people were screaming, 'Britney! Take pictures with me.' I just was like, 'Wow! This is huge!'"[4] Then, when he saw that Britney was going to be a guest on *The Tonight Show with Jay Leno,* he dressed up as her and sat in the audience. Of course, Jay and Britney noticed Derrick immediately and spoke to him from the stage, and that set the course for his future fame as a Britney Spears impersonator. In June 2004, he moved to Las Vegas and became the youngest cast member in the twenty-three-year history of "An Evening at La Cage" doing his Britney impersonation. In 2008, he competed on *America's Got Talent.* From there, he secured a coveted spot in the Divas Las Vegas female impersonator revue and began to tour the world performing as Britney.

Derrick continues to take risks and say yes to new opportunities. He starred as Britney in the video for Olivia Newton-John's remake of her own song "You Have to Believe." He had a small role in the USA Network's series *Dig.* In 2016, Derrick will be featured in an episode of "Graves," a comedy series on the cable channel EPIX, as well as the black action-comedy film *War on Everyone,* starring Alexander Skarsgård. As of this writing, he's been selected to appear on *RuPaul's Drag Race* Season 8.

When I interviewed Derrick, I just had the twinkle of an idea that I should do drag myself. I asked him for his advice: "Show up to your burlesque classes . . . show up to your lessons with your theater coach, and then you're eventually going to have to show up for your performance. That's it. The rest is going to happen."[5] He reminded me that I already knew a little about commanding a room. I am a keynote speaker after all. My first reaction was "Yeah, dude, but that's a lot different from cavorting around a nightclub stage in a giant wig, skimpy costume, and thigh-high boots lip-syncing for my life!" But I realized that during my drag performances, I could channel those times when I had shone on stage as a keynote speaker. Thank you for helping me see that, Derrick. So the next time you hesitate to take on something outside your comfort zone, remember Derrick's words: Just. Show. Up. The rest will take care of itself!

 **FROM EVERYDAY QUEENS**

How Shelly Stewart Kronbergs Went from a Self-Effacing Southern Sorority Girl to a Risk-Loving, Brazen Broad

So far, you have been reading Jackie's amazing stories, but we are going to switch now, and I (Shelly) am going to share my story of learning to take risks in life. And I must start by saying that I never imagined I would have a life that would be featured alongside those of drag queens and women of power!

I was raised to be a good girl in the heart of 1960s Texas—to say "Yes, ma'am" and "No, sir" to my mama and daddy and any other grown-up I encountered. I knew that children were to be seen and not heard. And I learned that being "the smart sister" took a back seat to being "the pretty sister." The dark side of all this conditioning, though, kept me silent during years of sexual abuse that began when I was eight and lasted until I was an adult. Even though I was smart as a child and liked being smart, southern culture teaches us that smart girls become smart women, and southern men aren't so keen on smart women. So by the time I got to college, I had learned to hide my smarts. Because if I didn't, how in the world was I going to get that coveted southern girl degree: the MRS?

So I followed all the culturally accepted guidelines. I was sweet to everybody I met. My braces came off just before my freshman year, and the college boys started to look my way. I joined a sorority (go Alpha Xi Delta!) and a philanthropy group called Angel Flight, which was a women's support organization (or girl groupies, as we called ourselves) for the Air Force ROTC fraternity Arnold Air Society. So far, so good. These guys were a little smarter than your average frat boy, and most of them were going to be pilots, which felt comfortable to me, as my daddy was a pilot and air-traffic controller. I almost slipped up, though, when I took an aerospace engineering elective that led to ground-school certification for a private pilot's license. I explored the possibility of actually becoming an Air Force pilot—I was twenty-fourth on the national list the year they decided to pick twenty-two women to go to pilot training. My scores on the exam were higher than those of almost all the young men on our campus. I lost some friends when I stopped pretending I wasn't smart, but I gained a husband who thought it was cool.

After we married, I followed him all over the world and had three lovely daughters before I turned twenty-nine. At every stage, my identity was boldly proclaimed on my military ID: D.W.—Dependent Wife, secondary citizen, adjunct life. I had a modicum of status as a pilot's wife, as the wife of the flight commander, then as the wife of an exchange pilot to Italy (OK, that was actually really cool), but it chafed at my growing need to be my own person. To do my own work. To have an ID that was just mine. And the work I started feeling called upon to do was something really hard and completely wrong for a girl who had been raised in the Southern Baptist Church. I wanted to be a spiritual leader. So as a way to break out of the cultural confinement, I decided to go to seminary.

I worried and prayed and wrestled with the idea that I was being called to be a Lutheran pastor. My children's dismay was just the beginning of the struggle. One day I sat them down at the kitchen table and said, "Girls, we are going to move home to Austin next summer so that I can go to school to be a pastor." Their silence was deafening. They all seemed to recoil a bit in their chairs. Finally, one of them said, "You mean you're going to be *up in front of everyone?*" The harsh reality of the spotlight that preachers' kids are under hit them, but eventually they were able to accept it. In fact, when my oldest went to college, she told me she gained a lot of feminist credibility because she had a mom who worked in a nongender-normative job. But it cost me, too. I discovered that my large, extended family didn't really accept a woman in this role. It turned out that their warmth didn't quite extend beyond their beliefs. That hurt. But I did it anyway.

I juggled being a hands-on mom with an airline pilot husband who was gone half of every month while I completed four years of graduate school, with three children in three different schools. It was the hardest thing I have ever done. Each child was as overscheduled as she could possibly be. I was the "Oh hell, let's just kick up soccer mom to a whole new level" kind of woman. Each of them was in a different scout troop, played a different instrument, and performed at school. And then there were the sports— volleyball, ice-skating, swim team, lacrosse, track, synchronized swimming (confession time: no one actually played soccer, but this counts, right?)—and some of these were select teams that competed nationally. Oh, and theater, and marching band, and color guard, and editing the freaking literary magazine. I was going crazy winning the stupid "mommy wars."

I graduated, became ordained, and served a small church on the outskirts of town. Until I couldn't anymore. You see, being a pastor is both a deeply satisfying and terribly restricting profession. I had the privilege of providing hope and love and encouragement to a group of people who opened up their lives and hearts to me. I got to speak and lead and teach, and I was finally, *finally*, celebrated for being smart. I loved these parts of the job. But those robes and that role began to chafe as much as the previous roles I'd played. Because the truth is, I am just not pious enough. I curse too much. I like to wear stiletto heels and low-cut blouses, and I really needed to be able to express my sexuality without leading a congregation off the skids. I also needed to make a change in my personal life, so when my twenty-eight-year marriage ended, I resigned.

I realized that I had still been circling the periphery of my self and my life. I needed to stop being the person everyone expected me to be and simply be me. I wanted to do the work I had loved as a pastor without concealing who I was in my life. Becoming a psychotherapist could give me both. Three more years of graduate school, followed by licensing exams, and I opened my private practice. The soul searching I did during this time helped me uncover one more aspect of myself that I had to explore. I wanted to get really comfortable with my sexual side. I had to make peace with the fact that, although I was the victim of sexual abuse, I still liked sex. With the help of my own psychotherapist, I began the hard task of healing. I gathered up my courage and started to date again and, on a whim, decided to take a burlesque dancing class.

I was fifty-one years old, and it was almost as intimidating as the first time I stepped into a pulpit to preach. But this time, instead of putting on robes and stoles, I was disrobing! In front of others! I was the oldest student by far, and probably the worst dancer, but I surprised myself by not caring. Because the most important thing I learned from burlesque is that the dancer is always in charge of what happens. The dancer can flirt and express her sexual side at her own pace. She can reveal what she chooses to reveal. She makes no promises in her dance other than that she enjoys it. Burlesque is about female empowerment, so I decided to pick a stage name that both reflected my newfound sense of power and respected my past history. I settled on Betty La Belle because it's an English spin on my favorite French fairy tale, *La Belle et la Bête*, better known as *Beauty and the Beast*, and that felt like a perfect fit for me. While I have performed burlesque many times in private, I won't do it in public and risk having one of my clients see it. That would violate the ethical standards of the counseling profession, which includes the absolute prohibition of any sexual relationship. So to strip off my clothes in front of a client even teasingly would come too close to being in that category. Not. Going. To. Happen.

I did do one somewhat public event that felt like taking a surprisingly big risk: I had a boudoir photo shoot done. I showed up at the studio with nothing more than a collection of sexy lingerie, heels, and my boyfriend's bass guitar. The photographer and the makeup artist did a great job of helping me feel at ease, even though I knew that my current body only slightly resembled the centerfold-worthy figure I had at twenty-one. I decided that my goal wasn't to be able to boast about my measurements or my long legs, but was to be able to claim the truth about my body: namely, that at that moment in time I was (and still am) a very sexy person.

I like being that. It's what got me to come out of the dressing room wearing that black-lace bra, stockings, stilettos, and a G-string made out of pearls, pose on the bearskin rug with that guitar between my stretched-out legs, and throw my head back and laugh. I had so much fun that they asked me to stay for another hour, and we took hundreds of pictures. I had the best ones made into a book as a reminder of how good it feels to take a risk and how much joy I feel in finally being me.

The things I experienced in the past—the suffering, the setbacks, the losses, and the struggles—no longer have the power to define me. I realized that, like these amazing drag queens, I get to define myself. And I choose to be more than just OK, more than just a survivor, more than just a "good girl." I choose, instead, to be the most fabulous, glorious self that I can be; to embrace my strength and power, and let the light of happiness and the joy of being fully, *fiercely* me shine forth.

 FROM THE COUCH

Risk Taking, Power Priming, and the Epigenetic Possibilities of Drag

Taking action is risky. Those action steps look good on paper and sound good in theory, but they sure are hard to actually do, aren't they? Especially for women. One of the reasons is simple physiology. Men have more of the risk-supporting testosterone than women do. And women have been acculturated to allow those differences to inhibit a lot of our impulses to take risks. But we are selling ourselves short, because we do possess *some* testosterone, and when we use it, really interesting things happen. In 2013, a research team in the Netherlands studied the differences in risk taking between males and females in puberty to determine the effects of testosterone and brain function in each gender. Each participant was able to click on a balloon pump to inflate it. Every time they clicked, they earned money, and they could cash out anytime they decided. But if the balloon popped before they chose to stop, they lost all their money. The scientists measured the testosterone levels of the participants as they made their choices. Unsurprisingly, the boys with higher testosterone popped more balloons. But much to their surprise, the girls with higher testosterone (compared to other girls) earned more money.[6] It turns out that there is a very high value for women to access and even increase their testosterone levels, and a compelling reason to do so.

How can you increase this hormone? Take charge of something! A team of researchers at the University of Michigan studied the effects of behavior—specifically, dominant behavior—on the levels of testosterone in men and women. They knew that the levels vary according to gender, but they discovered something else really interesting. Women's low levels of the hormone might actually be a result of being socialized not to express dominance. The study recruited men and women participants to act as a boss who is required to fire an employee in a business setting. Each person was asked to do this twice: the first time in a typically masculine or dominant fashion; the second, in a typically feminine or nondominant manner. The results showed very little difference in testosterone levels for men, but a significant increase in the levels for women, regardless of the manner in which they performed the task. They concluded that women could raise their testosterone levels simply by exercising power.[7] This study shows that to increase your level of testosterone, and therefore your ability to take risks, you just need to take charge of something—perhaps even take charge of what your next step, your next action, will be, and then do it.

When Pamela Barnes, former financial expert and current CEO of Engender Health, a global organization focused on women's health around the world, was asked what advice she would give to women who are hoping to rise to leadership in the business world, she replied: "For all professionals, and especially young women, the world outside our comfort zones can be huge and scary. Until we are willing to put ourselves out there and take a risk, we will never be able to achieve success and realize our potential. It's time to leave our comfort zone, time to go after what we're passionate about, and time to achieve our dreams."[8] To leave our comfort zone and go after our dreams, even when it feels like a big risk, is exactly what taking action, what *werking* is!

The ability to take risks and reach goals is vital to living a satisfying life. Edward Deci and Richard Ryan, the cofounders of the Self-Determination Theory, came to the realization that "one of the main trajectories in a person's life is to develop autonomy," which they understand as "acting from an integrated sense of self and endorsing one's own actions."[9] What they are saying is that life satisfaction is tied to the ways in which we choose what we do in life and that we like what we have chosen without needing outside approval for those choices. Self-determination is the act of choosing how our lives will go. It is the ultimate "take-charge" act that boosts testosterone and enables us to take the risks necessary to be the people we want to be.

The key, it seems, is to be willing to take a risk to do something that you love, that you care about, and that fills you with passion. The good news is that there are lots of techniques and methods that can help you do this. In addition to taking charge, another major way to increase risk taking is called "power priming." In 2012, a team of researchers from Europe and the United States conducted a series of experiments to determine the effects of priming a job or graduate school candidate with a memory of power. The first test involved participants who were randomly assigned the task of job applicant or interviewer. The applicants were then randomly given the task of either writing down a memory of when they had power or when they didn't have power in a situation in their lives. These letters were collected, and then the applicants filled out job applications, which were sent to interviewers who did not have access to the letters. The applicants who had written about a positive experience of having power in their lives were offered jobs at a significantly higher rate than both the control group, which did not have a writing assignment, and the group that wrote about an experience of having less power.

The researchers decided to see if this result held true in a face-to-face interview. So they gave the same writing assignment to university students who were participating in mock interviews for admission to graduate programs in the business school. They were manipulated into thinking that their writing assignment was done to assess handwriting, not to prime their brains for power. Their main task was to convince two interviewers, professors who were unaware of the power-prime assignment, to accept them into the program. These results were even more stunning: positive power priming increased the odds of being accepted by 81 percent compared to those in the control group, and 164 percent compared to those who had been negatively primed.[10] This is an incredibly powerful tool. All you need to do before an interview, a speech, or any potentially high-risk or high-stress event is take a few minutes beforehand to write down a moment when you were powerful, and the odds should always be in your favor.

The payoff for "werking it" might actually be more than just a successful, satisfying life. It might actually change the genetic code for you and your potential offspring. Which just might change the world. New research around this topic is happening in the field of epigenetics. Frances Champagne, a professor of psychology at Columbia University and prominent researcher of the relationship of epigenetics and social behavior, resilience, and heritability, discusses the basics of this new field and its implications in an article she wrote for the *Association for Psychological Science Observer* in 2009.[11] Epigenetics, she says, means the influences on a gene that are "in addition to genetic." We are learning that it isn't just the DNA itself that gets inherited; the way that the DNA can be arranged and accessed can also be inherited. What this might mean for you is that if you make a change in the way you manage stress, if you gain self-confidence, or if you increase your tolerance for risk taking, you could pass those behaviors down to your children through your DNA. There is also the possibility that if your children are exposed to parents who are changing the way they access their ability to be confident, then this might trigger the activation of that particular trait in the child and increase the probability of confidence being inherited in your child's future offspring. Champagne cautions that more studies are necessary to better understand this process, but she is confident that what scientists are learning about epigenetics will only support these findings. Just think, doing drag today could mean bolder children tomorrow!

notes FOR YOUR DRAG DIARY

You Better Werk!

If you haven't already gotten the message, this chapter is about getting out of your head, taking a risk, and moving forward with some action. True confidence is when you actually go through with doing something even though you may be afraid of the risks. If you can push yourself to take small risks, that will make it easier to try even bigger things next time. Keep trying new and bigger things by building on the success of those smaller challenges. So we have a question for you: Have you been breezing through this book, reading all of the Drag Diary homework but not doing any of the exercises? (Bonus points for those who have been trying things.) If you just haven't gotten around to doing those things, no worries. Now is your time! Did you think we would let you get away with not trying some new things, honey?

Take the **50 Days to Fierce Challenge**. How many of the Drag Diary homework items can you do in fifty days from the start of reading this book? Here's how you complete the challenge:

- Open your Drag Diary and write down the date.

- Start working your way through the list with the goal of completing all of the items in fifty days.

- For each item completed, first record how it felt to do the item in your Drag Diary. Then, on social media, post a photo or short video (less than fifteen seconds) related to the item with the hashtag #FiercelyYou and tagging me, @jackiehuba, on Twitter or Instagram.

- When your fifty days are up, tweet or post to Instagram a final celebratory message tagging @jackiehuba (again, on Twitter or Instagram) with the hashtags #FiercelyYou #FierceAtLast.

- If we find you have done all of the challenges, we will induct you into our drag family, the Haus of Fierce. All inductees will receive special Haus of Fierce recognition.

Does this list seem daunting? If so, recruit a friend to do it with you. Better yet, get a group of friends together as part of a book club and do it all together. Every time you meet, you can talk over your experience with each of the items.

You can do this. Now is your time to be fierce, fabulous, and more confident!

LIVING FIERCELY EVERY DAY

> **❝** *Pretend you're the best—point blank. When I'm in drag, I always say, 'They live in my world. I don't live in theirs.'* ["][1]

—Drag superstar Yara Sofia

We love this quote from Yara about others living in her world—a world where she is the star and everyone knows it. In this book, we call that world the Queendom, where we see ourselves as fabulous and fierce as seasoned drag queens, or better yet, we *are* queens. We know that it's not always easy to see ourselves this way. That is precisely why this idea of imaging oneself as one's fierce alter ego, who lives in a world of sequins and glitter, works. The campy, comedy queens I interviewed were especially insightful in this regard. Brian McCook is known around the world for his kooky drag alter ego, Katya Zamolodchikova, a self-described "average run-of-the-mill Russian bisexual trans-vestite hooker." He told me that in order to have the confidence to get on stage and pull off some of the zanier things he has done, he has to "say goodbye to any objective grip on reality and then just know that you're amazing. . . . You need that grip when you're [backstage] getting ready because you need to make sure that it looks all great and everything. You can't be delusional. But then [when you hit the stage], [you've] *got* to be delusional."[2] We just have to convince ourselves or, to use Katya's word, delude ourselves into believing that everyone is living in our world where we are freaking amazing. And they know it.

In this book, we've learned the Keys to Fierce: how to create a drag alter ego, how to dress and pose for power, how to shake off criticism, and how to take action outside our comfort zone. It's up to us to apply these lessons every day, no matter our profession or station in life. Laganja Estranja, a talented dancer, celebrity choreographer, and professional drag queen, told me, "I think a bank teller can be just as fierce as a drag queen. I really do believe that. In the way that they fold the dollars, in the way that they count it. Whatever it is, there's got to be a way to live your life fierce."[3]

Becoming Fiercely You

It's up to you now. We've invited you into the Queendom and we hope you will join us. Get out that Drag Diary and keep track of how you're doing, every step of the way, to become fiercely you. Share with us on social media your aha moments and your triumphs with the hashtag #FiercelyYou. Get information on *Fiercely You* drag transformation workshops, seminars, coaching, and makeovers at our HQ, EnterTheQueendom.com.

And for Pete's sake, go out and see some drag! Find the drag shows in your area and support your local queens. They'd love to see you, and your tips. Don't forget your dollar bills!

EPIL⊚GUE

....

DOING DRAG ON A TED STAGE

I've wanted to do a TED talk since the time that I (Jackie) became aware of what the organization was over twenty years ago. If you aren't familiar with them, TED events are a global set of conferences organized around the slogan "Ideas Worth Spreading." Speakers at these events are celebrated experts in their field, and past speakers at the exclusive main TED conference have included President Bill Clinton, Jane Goodall, Richard Dawkins, Bill Gates, Bono, and many Nobel Prize winners. TEDx events are independent TED-like events run by volunteer organizers in cities around the world, such as TEDxLosAngeles or TEDxLondon. Whether TED or TEDx, these are prestigious events, and being chosen to speak at one is quite an honor.

A few years ago, I had applied to a TEDx event for a city I don't want to name because I am about to throw some major shade at them. I filled out their extremely long and detailed application, explaining my idea for a talk on how to create confidence by thinking like a drag queen. I detailed my expertise, including my fourteen years of public speaking experience. I was even required to record a sixty-second video to outline the idea of how I hoped to inspire the audience with it. I felt my idea was unique, my experience was top-notch, and my video was well produced. To say I felt confident that I would be picked would be an understatement.

You can imagine my shock when I was rejected. I arranged a telephone call with one of the organizers of the event to help me understand why I hadn't made the cut. He told me that my idea was great, my years of speaking experience were unparalleled in comparison to the other applicants, and my video was on point. However, a drag queen (a man) had applied and was going to do a performance piece with his talk. The selection committee didn't want to have two talks on the subject of drag, so they went with a male drag queen because they were intrigued by his talk idea, and plus, I was told, "You're just a hobbyist, right? You're not a real drag queen." Oh, bitch! What did you just call me? Not. A. Real. Drag. Queen?! As we learned in Key Four with the female drag queens from London, women doing drag goes against the perception of what most people think drag queens are. Apparently that was the sentiment of this TEDx selection committee.

Pissed off but undeterred, I took my talk idea and immediately applied to another TEDx event. I had all the information I had used for the last application, including the video. Applying online for this event was a breeze. Surely this group of people would get what I was trying to do. I was excited anew! And yet I was rejected again. I didn't bother to ask for a phone conversation with someone from the selection committee to explain the rejection, because at this point it just didn't matter. I felt dejected and defeated. My TED talk aspirations were dashed.

To my complete surprise, a year later one of the organizers of TEDxVancouver e-mailed me about a speaking opportunity. The selection committee had heard about me from one of my speaking clients and was inquiring if I would be interested in delivering a talk related to my customer loyalty book on Lady Gaga. This was my big chance! When I spoke to the contact on the phone, I asked what the theme of the conference was, and she said "Identity." Could this be any more perfect? She was open to hearing about other topics related to this that I might speak on, and I pitched the idea of creating a fierce persona like drag queens do that you can channel when you need confidence. She loved it! I had found my people, my tribe! They got me. She explained that this TEDx event was expected to be one of the biggest in the world, with over thirty-five hundred people in Vancouver's Rogers Arena where the National Hockey League Canucks play. Wow!

This was a big stage to fill. I felt like I couldn't stand up there talking for twelve minutes about how I became a female drag queen without actually doing some drag! So I concocted this crazy idea to do a short one-minute drag routine at the end of my twelve-minute talk. This would involve doing the entire talk in normal everyday drag with a real drag costume underneath, because I wanted to demonstrate visually that I always have my fierce drag persona inside me. I would have to wear a wig that looked like my real hair on top of a long straight red wig curled up underneath. I would wear a professional-looking navy pin-stripe suit that would tear away to reveal a long-sleeve silver-and-black shimmering sequin catsuit. Near the end of the talk, I would peel off what (hopefully) looked like my real hair to reveal the red wig. Then four hot male backup dancers would run in and pull off the business suit, which would tear away into four pieces.

Perfecting a memorized twelve-minute talk on a topic that I'd never presented before, in front of thirty-five hundred people (and soon on YouTube forever) was daunting enough. Adding the complexity of a drag routine was just insane. In order to pull this off, I would have to fly *six* people (a choreographer, four dancers, and a makeup/costume stylist, aka my drag mother, Kelly) to Vancouver. I decided to bring the choreographer so that he could make any changes to the routine if we needed to once we practiced on the actual stage. Plus, what if something happened to one of my dancers? This was too important an opportunity to have something go wrong and lose a dancer, which would compromise the performance. The choreographer could fill the dancer's spot if needed. I began to think this was going to be the most expensive talk in TED history!

I had exactly three months to make all of this happen. First I had to craft the talk itself. Creating a twelve-minute talk is infinitely harder than my normal keynotes, which are usually forty-five minutes to an hour long. It's hard to get all of your points across in such a short time. I worked via Skype with my longtime speaking coach Victoria Labalme, who's located in New York City, to put the outline of the talk together. Then I spent hours and hours fine-tuning the talk with Austin-based speaking coach Barbara Miller in one-on-one sessions and practice runs in front of small live audiences. I had at least four feedback sessions with the TEDxVancouver folks, who made changes to my outline and talk. But making the drag routine happen was a whole other beast.

There were times during these three months when I was just exhilarated! My creative juices were flowing. I was practicing my dance routine with world-class dancers. The costume reveal was killer. My crazy idea was coming to life. But that didn't stop my inner critic Felicia from making me doubt my ability to do this. Felicia would say things like, "This is the dumbest idea in TED history. TED is for serious issues like how schools kill creativity, racial injustice in

America, and why domestic violence victims don't leave their abusers. And you're talking about drag queens?" Felicia would also ruminate on worst-case scenarios of what could happen: "What if the costume reveal doesn't work? What if you forget the choreography, or worse, your talking points? What if you freeze up, like you did at the Austin International Drag Festival?" Yikes! I knew that the risks I had taken before had paid off. I was *committed* to the idea of helping people know that you can channel power by thinking like a drag queen, and of being the first person to present it in this prestigious venue. I was determined to make this happen! So I told Miss Felicia to sashay away and not to let the door hit her on the way out.

I won't take you through all the trials and tribulations (there were a lot of them) of finally getting the whole thing together and making it to Vancouver. I just know that before walking out on that stage, I was the most nervous I have ever been in my entire life. Yes, even more than at the dang Austin International Drag Festival. When it was my turn, I made it out onto the stage. I could barely make out any of the faces in the audience in the dark arena with the bright spotlights in my face. I began to speak and . . . eek! All of the moisture in my mouth instantly evaporated. I was making that dry-mouth clicking sound when I spoke. What the hell? I couldn't believe it. This was my moment. I had prepared— strike that—I had overprepared for any problem that might arise. But I hadn't expected this to happen. It had never happened in all my fourteen years of speaking. I just had to muddle through. But luckily that was really the only thing that went awry. I nailed most of my speaking points. The audience let out a collective loud gasp followed by thunderous applause when the costume reveal happened. The dancers performed perfectly. I'll let you watch the video to see what you think of how I did. (Go to EntertheQueendom .com/videos to see the talk.) But the tweet from the TEDx-Vancouver Twitter account after my talk made it all worthwhile. It said simply: "@jackiehuba / @LadyTrinity just blew our minds!"[1]

This adventure into the world of drag has changed my life. Besides the most important benefit of being transformed into the fiercest version of myself, it has led me to a life goal that I wasn't sure I would ever achieve: doing a TED talk. Over the course of a few years, I went from performing in front of a few folks in my burlesque class to performing in front of thirty-five hundred people at a TED event (plus countless people watching the YouTube video). I pushed myself to try new things outside my comfort zone and work through my fears. Had I talked myself out of this crazy idea of becoming a female drag queen, none of this would have happened. I believe this is a true life lesson of how taking risks, and working through fears, can lead you to the things you want to achieve in life. Now I'm excited to use my story and the lessons I've learned to help people become fiercely themselves.

And what is the future for Lady Trinity? Well, she will continue to inspire me to take chances and be bold, whether I perform as her or not. She will always be a part of me. But you can be sure that if the occasion presents itself, she will *turn the party* in her supermodel hair, sequined catsuit, and stiletto boots. Werk!

A DRAG PRIMER

Know Your *Her*story

Drag queens have a long and storied history, and it's important for the context of this book that you not only know the background information but how important drag queens are to the entire LGBT community.

THE ORIGINS OF DRAG

History is a bit unclear on where the term "drag" came from, although many attribute it to Shakespearean theater where women were not permitted to act on stage, men played the female roles "DRessed As a Girl," and "drag" is an acronym for this.

Perhaps the first well-known American drag performer was Julian Eltinge, who began performing in drag at age ten. In 1904, at age twenty-three, he was appearing on Broadway in drag. In 1910, at the height of his drag fame, he went on a national tour of America and produced his own magazines, one of which was aimed at his sizeable female audience and shared beauty hints and tips.

CATEGORIES OF DRAG

There are as many styles of drag as there are colors of nail polish. Some of the more prominent drag styles include:

- High drag, which is based on clownish devices such as exaggeration, satire, and ribaldry. Everything is over-the-top—big boobs, big hair, big hips, and so on.

- *Fishy*, in which queens attempt to look as much as possible like real women in their makeup and clothing.

- Pageant queens are queens who compete regularly in drag pageants. A drag pageant is very similar to a female beauty pageant, with judged categories that include gown, talent, and onstage questions.

- Celebrity impersonators are queens who perform in the style of a specific celebrity. Sometimes resorting to plastic surgery, they aim to act and look like the star they are portraying. Favorite personalities for celebrity impersonators include Cher, Madonna, Tina Turner, Liza Minnelli, Reba McIntyre, and Barbra Streisand.

- Skag drag is a style of drag where queens do not attempt to hide their male appearance. Although they use makeup and may wear a dress, they may also sport a full beard and expose their hairy beer belly.

- Postmodernist drag queens, "tranimal," or "terrorist drag" mix performance art, punk rock, and racial and social issues into drag. Many of these types of queens often use unkempt wigs and clothing.

- Camp queens go for the comedy angle. This can be showcased in their makeup, costumes, performance, or any mix of these.

Drag has also long been part of pop culture in movies, television, music, and theater. Some of the more prominent recent examples of this include:

- Music, like Madonna's 1990 number-one song "Vogue," which showcased voguing, a style of dance popularized in the New York City drag ball scene, and of course, RuPaul's 1992 dance hit "Supermodel."

- Television, including the Tom Hanks' vehicle *Bosom Buddies* and *RuPaul's Drag Race,* now in its eighth season, the most popular show on MTV's LOGO network.

- Movies: *The Bird Cage, To Wong Foo Thanks for Everything, Julie Newmar,* and Tyler Perry's eight movies portraying his Madea character.

- Broadway: Tony award–winning shows such as *Hedwig and the Angry Inch,* and *Kinky Boots.*

DRAG QUEENS' ROLE IN THE FIGHT FOR LGBT RIGHTS

After World War II, Wisconsin senator Joseph McCarthy stoked national paranoia in America. What does this have to do with drag? Well, anything that was deemed "subversive" (e.g., the Communist Party, homosexuals) was also thought of as a risk to the country. In the 1950s, the FBI began tracking "known homosexuals," even posting their names in local newspapers. The wearing of opposite-gender clothes was banned, and gay men and women were often publicly humiliated, harassed, fired from jobs, jailed, or institution-alized. Police began raiding gay establishments in cities across the country, revoking liquor licenses and arresting patrons. Anyone with an ID was booked and released; anyone without an ID was arrested, as well as anyone who wasn't wearing at least three pieces of clothing that matched their sex.

The Stonewall Inn was the only gay bar in New York City, and in 1969 it became the birthplace of the modern gay rights movement. Raids became increasingly frequent in the summer of 1969, and finally, on June 28th of that year, the patrons were pushed too far. At 1:20 a.m. on that fateful day, the police raid did not go as planned. For the first time, the patrons fought back. Many believe riots were instigated after drag queen Sylvia Rivera threw pennies and quarters at police. Three nights of riots ensued, which included another drag queen, Marsha P. Johnson, smashing a police car window with her purse.

This was the first time LGBT people had protested as a community. The events at Stonewall ignited widespread, worldwide protests. In 1970, to mark the first anniversary of the Stonewall uprisings, the very first Gay Pride marches took place in New York, Los Angeles, San Francisco, and Chicago. Drag queens were instrumental in the first fight to gain equality for the LGBT community and should be celebrated as such.

WANT TO LEARN EVEN MORE ABOUT DRAG *HER*STORY?

Here's a list of some important films and documentaries for you to peruse:

- *Paris Is Burning*: the seminal 1990 documentary film by Jennie Livingston on drag ball culture in New York City.

- *Pay It No Mind: The Life and Times of Marsha P. Johnson*: a documentary film about the legendary transgender drag queen activist. As of this writing, it is only available on YouTube.

- *Pageant*: a documentary film that showcases the world of drag pageants.

- *I Am Divine*: a documentary film about how Harris Glenn Milstead became John Waters's cinematic muse and an international drag icon.

GLOSSARY OF DRAG TERMS

Beating your face: To apply the perfect amount of makeup on the face, resulting in a flawless look, i.e., "her face is beat for the gods."

Busted (adj.): The act of appearing to be unkempt, messy, unrefined, unpolished, or poorly presented.

Bye Felicia: An expression used to dismiss someone. This person is usually irrelevant and annoying. The term is a reference from the film *Friday*.

Clock (v.): (a) To spot what someone is trying to hide; (b) to call out a person's flaws; (c) to uncover or reveal the truth in a situation. For example, "You cannot clock that mug," or "Phi Phi clocked Willam for his five o'clock shadow."

Condragulations: The drag queen version of "congratulations."

Death drop (n.): A fall, drop, or descent backward onto one's back with one's leg folded underneath, in dramatic style. Usually part of a dance routine. This move is part of the voguing style of dance.

Drag daughter (n.): *See* Drag mother.

Drag mother (n.): Also *drag daughter, drag family*. An experienced drag performer who acts as a mentor and guide to someone who wants to learn the art of drag. Often, the new drag queen, who is referred to as the drag mother's drag daughter, takes the last name of her drag mother to pay homage to her. A drag family is made up of a drag mother and all of her drag daughters.

Dusted (adj.): The act of looking polished, flawless, or perfect. The opposite of "busted."

Feeling the fantasy: The giddy feeling you get when you absolutely love what you are doing in a particular moment.

Fishy: A term used to describe a drag queen who looks extremely feminine or one who convincingly resembles a biological woman. The term refers to the supposed scent of a woman's vagina, which is colloquially likened to the smell of fish. (As feminists, we don't love this word, but drag doesn't take itself seriously, so we shouldn't either. Besides, fish is healthy and delicious.)

For the gods (adv.): Abbreviated use of the phrase "fit for the gods," used to qualify an act done perfectly or flawlessly—e.g., (a) "Her face is painted for the gods," (b) "That dress is clinging to her like a second skin because it is tailored for the gods."

Gag (v.): To react intensely, usually as a result of shock; may also be used as an exclamation—e.g., "I am gagging on that three-foot-high wig!"

Giving me life: A phrase that shows how much you enjoy something.

The house down: Another term used for an exclamation point at the end of a sentence to indicate how extra fabulous something is—e.g., "Kennedy is dancing the house down." Another usage is *the house-down boots.*

Hunty (n.): A contraction of the terms "honey" and "cunt," used as a term of endearment among drag queens.

Kai kai (n.): The circumstance in which drag queens engage in sexual activity. Not to be confused with *kiki.*

Kiki (n.): A term used for gossip, small talk, chatting, or a heart-to-heart.

Let them have it!: A phrase that refers to impressing people with your fabulous drag.

The library is open: A phrase announcing that a queen is about to share some criticisms about another person or queen. These criticisms are known as *reads*. See Reading.

Mug (n.): A queen's face.

No tea, no shade: A phrase meaning "No disrespect."

Paint (v.): To apply makeup to one's face—e.g., "It takes two hours to paint my mug."

Reading (v.): To wittily and incisively expose a person's flaws (e.g., "read them like a book"), often exaggerating or elaborating on them; an advanced form of the insult. Another usage is to *read someone to filth*, which just means that you are being extra nasty with your insults.

Realness (n.): A likeness that is deemed to be as close as possible to a specific category or genre—e.g., "She is serving warrior princess realness."

Serve (v.): To present oneself in a certain way. See Realness.

Shade (n.): The casting of aspersions. A form of insult. Subtly pointing out a person's flaws or faults. Derived from the term "reading"—e.g., "I don't tell you you're ugly, but I don't have to tell you because you know you're ugly," a quote from the movie *Paris Is Burning*.

Shady (adj.): Possessing a blunt and insulting manner.

Sickening (adj.): Incredibly amazing; excessively hot.

Slay (v.): To achieve something spectacular. Sometimes also written as *slay the children* with the same meaning.

Tea (n.): A back-formation from the letter *T* for "truth"; refers to gossip, news, information, or true facts, e.g., "What's the tea?"

Throwing shade: The act of criticism delivered in a blunt and insulting manner, e.g., "Tyra was throwing shade at the other queens on the show."

Tuck (v.): To arrange one's male genitalia in a way that they are not visible so that one resembles a woman; (n.) the result of a man containing his genitalia (typically with duct tape and multiple pairs of pantyhose) so that they are not visible.

Turn the party: To captivate, enthrall, and overwhelm an audience with one's fabulosity.

Werk (v.): (a) A term meaning to "work your body"; (b) to strut, especially on the runway; (c) to give an outstanding presentation.

NOTES

INTRODUCTION

1. Den Renzi, "The 8 Nastiest Reality TV Villains," *Huffington Post,* April 4, 2012, http://www.huffingtonpost.com /dan-renzi/reality-tv-villains_b_1450314.html (accessed December 13, 2015).

THE NEED FOR FIERCE

1. Katty Kay and Claire Shipman, "The Confidence Gap," *The Atlantic,* May 2014 issue, http://www.theatlantic.com /magazine/archive/2014/05/the-confidence-gap/359815 (accessed March 31, 2016).

2. Julie Coffman and Bill Neuenfeldt, "Everyday Moments of Truth: Frontline Managers Are Key to Women's Career Aspirations," Bain & Company INSIGHTS report, June 17, 2014, http://www.bain.com/publications/articles/everyday -moments-of-truth.aspx (accessed March 31, 2016).

3. Williamson, *Return to Love: Reflections on the Principles of a Course in Miracles* (New York: Harper Collins, 1992), 190.

4. *Oxford Dictionaries: Language Matters,* "Fierce," http:// www.oxforddictionaries.com/us/definition/american _english/fierce (accessed February 6, 2016).

5. *Urban Dictionary,* "Fierce," http://www.urbandictionary .com/define.php?term=Fierce (accessed February 6, 2016).

LEARN FROM THE QUEENS OF FIERCE

1. RuPaul, "Introduction," in *Workin' It!* (New York: Harper-Collins e-books, 2009), Kindle ed.

THE FIRST KEY

1. Ella Walker, "Launching new drag acts is my legacy and I'm so proud," *Belfast Telegraph,* February 6, 2016, http://www.belfasttelegraph.co.uk/life/features/launching -new-drag-acts-is-my-legacy-and-im-so-proud-34421058 .html (accessed March 29, 2016).

2. Michael Schulman, "In Drag, It Turns Out, There Are Second Acts," *New York Times,* February 21, 2014, http:// www.nytimes.com/2014/02/23/fashion/RuPaul-Drag-Race -television.html (accessed December 12, 2015).

3. RuPaul, interview by Arsenio Hall, *The Arsenio Hall Show,* Season 6, Episode 68, syndicated by CBS, December 16, 1993.

4. April Carrión, in-person interview with the author, July 5, 2014.

5. Courtney Constable, "5 Things I Learned from Drag Queens," *Courtney Conquers: All Dragged Up,* October 28, 2015, https://courtneyconquersblog.wordpress.com/2015 /10/28/10-things-i-learned-from-drag-queens (accessed December 12, 2015).

6. Eric Spitznagel, "Drag Queens, High Heels, and Delicious Squirrels: An Interview with Dolly Parton," Ericspitznagel .com, June 29, 2014, http://www.ericspitznagel.com /suddeutsche-zeitung-magazin/dolly-parton/ (accessed November 6, 2015).

7. Laura Cox, "The town tramp inspired my trashy look because I was a plain Jane, says Dolly Parton," *Daily Mail,* December 10, 2012, http://www.dailymail.co.uk/tvshowbiz /article-2246206/Dolly-Parton-The-town-tramp-inspired -trashy-look.html#ixzz3qm4zc1E8 (accessed November 6, 2015).

8. "Dolly Parton: I got style inspiration from a hooker," *Now Magazine,* March 25, 2007, http://www.nowmagazine.co .uk/celebrity-news/celebrity-gossip-dolly-parton-i-got -style-inspiration-from-a-prostitute-239299 (accessed November 6, 2015).

9. Dolly Parton, Twitter post, July 12, 2010, 10:26 a.m., http://twitter.com/DollyParton.

10. Z100 radio station website, "Lady Gaga In-Studio," interview with host Elvis Duran, August 20, 2013, http://www.z100.com/articles/z100-news-451815/lady-gaga -instudio-11586429 (accessed November 6, 2015).

11. Devin Dwyer, "President Obama Calls Lady Gaga 'A Little Intimidating,'" *ABC News*, October 3, 2011, http://abcnews .go.com/blogs/politics/2011/10/president-obama-calls-lady -gaga-a-little-intimidating/ (accessed November 7, 2015).

12. Gina Pace, "Beyonce's Alter Ego," *Associated Press*, October 5, 2005, http://www.cbsnews.com/news/beyonces -alter-ego/ (accessed November 7, 2015).

13. Lyrics for "Diva" from the album *I Am . . . Sasha Fierce*, http://www.beyonce.com/album/i-am-sasha-fierce/ (accessed November 7, 2015).

14. "Beyoncé Tells Fans to Call Her by Alter-Ego 'Sasha Fierce,'" FoxNews.com, October 23, 2008, http://www .foxnews.com/story/2008/10/23/beyonce-tells-fans-to-call -her-by-alter-ego-sasha-fierce.html (accessed November 7, 2015).

15. "Beyoncé Knowles: Queen B," *The Independent*, September 21, 2001, http://www.independent.co.uk/news/people /profiles/beyonceacute-knowles-queen-b-414158.html (accessed November 7, 2015).

16. Coco Montrese, in-person interview with the author, September 17, 2013.

17. Interview with Larry Flick for OutQ Radio on SiriusXM Entertainment, August 10, 2014. https://soundcloud.com /siriusxmentertainment/adore-delano-is-daniel-noriegas -super-hero (accessed November 9, 2015).

18. "Sissy That Walk," *RuPaul's Drag Race*, Season 6, Episode 12, air date May 5, 2014, 12:39.

19. Danny Noriega (aka Adore Delano), telephone interview with the author, July 5, 2014.

20. Connie Wang, "Meet Baddie Winkle, Who Fell in Love with Raver Clothes at Age 87," Refinery29.com, September 2, 2015, http://www.refinery29.com/baddie-winkle# .pyzha8:C7tz (accessed November 9, 2015).

21. Tess Koman, "Baddie Winkle: All the College Kids Just Want Me to Be Their Grandma," *Cosmopolitan*, http:// www.cosmopolitan.com/entertainment/celebs/a39902 /baddie-winkle-internets-most-fascinating (accessed December 12, 2015).

22. Wang, "Meet Baddie Winkle."

23. Ibid.

24. Ibid.

25. Marc Cuenco, "86-Year-Old Baddie Winkle Stars in DimePiece Ad Campaign Promoting Timeless Female Empowerment," Bustle.com, April 7, 2015, http://www .bustle.com/articles/74824-86-year-old-baddie-winkle -stars-in-dimepiece-ad-campaign-promoting-timeless -female-empowerment (accessed November 9, 2015).

26. Miley Cyrus, Instagram post, April 6, 2015, 5:18pm, https://instagram.com/p/1J0AthwzG4/.

27. Wang, "Meet Baddie Winkle."

28. C. G. Jung, *The Essential Jung,* ed. A. Storr (Princeton, NJ: Princeton University Press, 1983), 94.

29. D. Beau (2014), "Week 10: Guest Speaker—Dickie Beau," DRAM10002 *Theatre and Performance: Concepts.*

30. Carol S. Dweck, "Can Personality Be Changed? The Role of Beliefs in Personality and Change," *Current Direction in Psychological Science* 17, no. 6 (December 2008): 391–394.

31. Jaye L. Derrick, Shira Gabriel, and Brooke Tippin, "Para-social Relationships and Self-Discrepancies: Faux Relationships Have Benefits for Low Self-Esteem Individuals," *Personal Relationships* 15, issue 2 (2008): 261–280.

THE SECOND KEY

1. *Trenton Evening Times*, Section: Family Weekly (newspaper supplement), "Ask Them Yourself: Question for Bette Midler," unnumbered page: second page of section, January 13, 1980, Trenton, NJ.

2. Jase Peeples, "RuPaul's *Drag Race* Alums Share Lessons Drag Can Teach the World," *Advocate*, May 20, 2014, http://www.advocate.com/arts- entertainment/people/2014/05/20/rupauls-drag-race-alums-share-lessons-drag-can-teach-world (accessed December 13, 2015).

3. Kelly Kline, in-person interview with the author, August 19, 2013.

4. Facebook, Kelly Kline, July 21, 2014, https://www.facebook.com/KellyKline512/posts/10152216205710036.

5. *RuPaul's Drag Race*, "The Fabulous Bitch Ball," Season 4, Episode 11, directed by Nick Murray, LOGO, April 9, 2012.

6. Kyle Munzenrieder, "Latrice Royale: Drag Royalty," *Miami New Times*, November 22, 2012 (accessed November 22, 2015).

7. *RuPaul's Drag Race*, "Reunion," Season 4, Episode 14, directed by Nick Murray, LOGO, April 30, 2012.

8. Latrice Royale, telephone interview with the author, August 21, 2013.

9. Anelica Mark-Harris, in-person interview with the authors, August 20, 2015.

10. Ibid.

11. Ibid.

12. Ibid.

13. Ibid.

14. Bessie Mark-Dillard, in-person interview with the authors, August 20, 2015.

15. Arletha Phillips, in-person interview with the authors, August 20, 2015.

16. Christina Harris, in-person interview with the authors, August 20, 2015.

17. Ibid.

18. Ibid.

19. Anelica Mark-Harris, in-person interview with the authors, August 20, 2015.

20. Hajo Adam and Adam D. Galinsky, "Enclothed Cognition," *Journal of Experimental Social Psychology* (2012), doi:10.1016/j.jesp.2012.02.008.

21. PT Staff, "Tall People Get Paid More," *Psychology Today*, published on October 20, 2003, last reviewed on March 5, 2008, https://www.psychologytoday.com/articles/200310 /tall-people-get-paid-more (accessed October 2, 2015). See also Timothy A. Judge, "The Effect of Physical Height on Workplace Success and Income: Preliminary Test of a Theoretical Model," *Journal of Applied Psychology* 89, no. 3 (2004): 428–441.

22. Christina Tsaousi, "Consuming Underwear: Fashioning Female Identity" (PhD diss., University of Leicester, 2011).

23. Hayley Phelan, "Margaret Thatcher Set the Bar for Power Dressing," *Fashionista*, April 8, 2013, http://fashionista .com/2013/04/margaret-thatcher-set-the-bar-for-power -dressing (accessed October 10, 2015).

24. Laura Abassi, "'Their Image of Me': A Phenomenological Study of Professional Dress Choices of Female Professors," *Proceedings of the New York State Communication Association,* vol. 2012, art. 4 (2013).

25. Janelle Manton, "Power Dressing at Work," *Top Secret Women's Business*, April 8, 2012, http:// topsecretwomensbusiness.com/power-dressing-at-work (accessed November 28, 2015).

26. Irene Scott, telephone interview with the author, November 20, 2015.

27. Ibid.

28. Ibid.

29. Miss Fame, in-person interview with the author, August 10, 2015.

THE THIRD KEY

1. Courtney Act, in-person interview with the author, September 3, 2014.

2. Jennifer Demartino and Richard A. Gradone, "Amazing" lyrics, *Sprechen Sie Hi Fashion?* R Gradone Music/Silver tooth, 2011.

3. D. J. Pierce, in-person interview with the author, September 9, 2013.

4. Ibid.

5. Jujubee, in-person interview with the author, August 18, 2013.

6. Ibid.

7. Ibid.

8. Brendan Jordan, in-person interview with the author, May 20, 2015.

9. Ibid.

10. Ibid.

11. Ibid.

12. Ibid.

13. Ibid.

14. Ibid.

15. John F. Dovidio and Steve L. Ellyson, "Decoding Visual Dominance: Attributions of Power Based on Relative Percentages of Looking While Speaking and Looking While Listening," *Social Psychology Quarterly* 45 (1982): 106–113.

16. Laura Z. Tiedens and Alison R. Fragale, "Power Moves: Complementarity in Dominant and Submissive Nonverbal

Behavior," *Journal of Personality and Social Psychology* 84 (2003): 558–568.

17. Dana R. Carney, Amy J. C. Cuddy, and Andy J. Yap, "Power Posing: Brief Nonverbal Displays Affect Neuroendocrine Levels and Risk Tolerance," *Psychological Science Online First,* September 21, 2010.

18. Serena Chen, Annette Y. Lee-Chai, and John A. Bargh, "Relationship Orientation as a Moderator of the Effects of Social Power," *Journal of Personality and Social Psychology* 80 (2001): 173–187.

19. Shelly Taylor, "Friend and Befriend Theory," in *Handbook of Theories of Social Psychology,* ed. Paul A. M. Van Lange, Arie W. Kruglanski, and E. Tory Higgins (London: Sage Publications, 2012), 13–28.

20. Miss Fame, in-person interview with the author, August 10, 2015.

21. Rich Jurzwiak, "Enter Cookie: An Empire Supercut," Gawker.com, January 29, 2015, http://morningafter.gawker .com/enter-cookie-an-empire-supercut-1682641678 (accessed December 5, 2015).

THE FOURTH KEY

1. *Paris Is Burning,* film; Jennie Livingston, Off White Productions, 1990.

2. Tara Mohr, "Learning to Love Criticism," *New York Times,* September 27, 2014, http://www.nytimes.com/2014/09/28 /opinion/sunday/learning-to-love-criticism.html (accessed December 8, 2015).

3. Patrick Farabaugh, "Welcome to the Dollhouse," *Our Lives Magazine,* January 2015, http://ourlivesmadison.com /article/welcome-to-the-dollhouse (accessed December 3, 2015).

4. Zach Brooke, "Q&A: Trixie Mattel," *Milwaukee Magazine,* September 8, 2015, http://www.milwaukeemag.com/2015 /09/08/qa-trixie-mattel (accessed December 3, 2015).

5. Brian Firkus (aka Trixie Mattel), in-person interview with the author, April 5, 2015.

6. Ibid.

7. Ibid.

8. Broadly Staff, "Can't Drag Us Down: Meet London's Female Queens," *Broadly*, September 15, 2015, https://broadly.vice.com/en_us/video/cant-drag-us-down-meet-londons-female-queens (accessed December 2, 2015).

9. Ibid.

10. Holly Falconer and Nell Frizell, "Glitter Beards, Cleavage and Gender Fucking: A Day with London's Female Drag Queens," *Vice*, November 14, 2014, http://www.vice.com/en_uk/read/londons-faux-queens (accessed December 2, 2015).

11. Broadly Staff, "Can't Drag Us Down."

12. Rosalind Wiseman, *Queen Bees and Wannabes: Helping Your Daughter Survive Cliques, Gossip, Boyfriends, and the New Realities of Girl World* (2002), 2nd ed. (New York: Three Rivers Press, 2009), 164.

13. Daniel Goleman, *Social Intelligence: The New Science of Human Relationships* (New York: Bantam Books, 2006), 114.

14. Ibid., 231.

15. Susan Nolan-Hoeksema, Blair E. Wisco, and Sonya Lyubormiskey, "Rethinking Rumination," *Perspectives on Psychological Science* 3, no. 5 (2008), 400.

16. Ibid.

17. Dudley Clendinen and Adam Nagourney, *Out for Good: The Struggle to Build a Gay Rights Movement in America* (New York: Simon & Schuster, 1999), 529.

1. Neal Strauss, "The Broken Heart and Violent Fantasies of Lady Gaga," *Rolling Stone,* July 8, 2010, http://www .rollingstone.com/music/news/the-broken-heart-and -violent-fantasies-of-lady-gaga-20100708 (accessed December 9, 2015).

2. Cynthia Lee Fontaine, in-person interview with the author, December 7, 2015.

3. Derrick Barry, in-person interview with the author, September 16, 2013.

4. Ibid.

5. Ibid.

6. Jiska S. Peper, P. Cedric, M. P. Koolschijn, and Evelyn A. Crone, "Development of Risk Taking: Contributions of Adolescent Testosterone and Orbital-frontal Cortex," *Journal of Cognitive Neuroscience* 25, no. 12 (December 2013): 2141–2150.

7. Sari M. van Anders, Jeffrey Steiger, and Katherine L. Goldey, "Effects of Gendered Behavior on Testosterone in Women and Men," *Proceedings of the National Academy of Sciences* (2015), doi: 10.1073/pnas.1509591112.

8. Carrie Murphy, "CEO Pamela Barnes of Global Women's Health Nonprofit GenderHealth Talks Career Changes and Taking Risks," interview with Pamela Barnes, *The Grindstone,* June 28, 2013, http://www.thegrindstone.com /2013/06/28/education/female-ceo-engender-health -pamela-barnes/#ixzz2bmvaW0zH (accessed December 8, 2015).

9. Edward L. Deci and Richard M. Ryan, "The 'What' and 'Why' of Goal Pursuits: Human Needs and the Self-Determination of Behavior," *Psychological Inquiry* 11, no. 4 (2000): 227–268.

10. Joris Lammers, David Dubois, Derek D. Rucker, and Adam D. Galinsky, "Power Gets the Job: Priming Power Increases Interview Outcomes," *Journal of Experimental*

Social Psychology (2013), http://dx.doi.org/10:1016/j.jesp
.2013.2.008.

11. Frances A. Champagne, "Beyond Nature vs. Nurture: Philosophical Insights from Molecular Biology," *Association for Psychological Science Observer* 22, no. 4 (April 2009), http://www.psychologicalscience.org/index.php /publications/observer/2009/april-09/beyond-nature-vs -nurture-philosophical-insights-from-molecular-biology .html (accessed April 6, 2016).

CONCLUSION

1. J. R. Tongol, "RuPaul, Sharon Needles, Raja, Lady Bunny and Other Drag Queens Offer Up Life Lessons," *Huffington Post,* February 4, 2013, http://www.huffingtonpost.com /2013/02/04/drag-queen-wisdom_n_2593829.html (accessed December 10, 2015).

2. Brian McCook (aka Katya Zamolodchikova), in-person interview with the author, April 23, 2015.

3. Laganja Estranja, in-person interview with the author, September 10, 2015.

EPILOGUE

1. TEDxVancouver, Twitter post, November 14, 2015, 7:34 p.m., http://twitter.com/tedxvancouver.

ACKNOWLEDGMENTS

JOINT ACKNOWLEDGMENTS

Our thanks go to the many people who were part of this book project: the folks at our stupendous publisher, Berrett-Koehler: Neal Maillet, our editor, and Jeevan Sivasubramaniam, managing director, for believing in this book and loving the concept as much as we did. To the rest of our team at Berrett-Koehler—Charlotte Ashlock, Maria Jesús Auiló, Shabnam Banerjee-McFarland, Marina Cook, Michael Crowley, Matt Fagaly, Kristen Frantz, David Marshall, Edward Wade, and Lasell Whipple—who so brilliantly contributed their expertise to bringing the book to the world.

To Kate Sage, our developmental editor, who shepherded our piecemeal work into a finished manuscript, and who as our project manager kicked our butts when she needed to.

To all of the drag queens who took time out of their crazy schedules to share their wisdom with us: Courtney Act, Derrick Barry, April Carrión, Adore Delano, Laganja Estranja, Miss Fame, Cynthia Lee Fontaine, Jujubee, Trixie Mattel, Chad Michaels, Coco Montrese, Phi Phi O'Hara, Raven, Latrice Royale, Yara Sofia, Shangela Laquifa Wadley, and Katya Zamolodchikova. Thank you as well to Chris Liporto and David Charpentier and everyone at Producer Entertainment for your support of this project.

To Bernadette Jiwa, master storytelling sage, for crafting our brilliant title. To Erin Tyler, our talented cover designer, and Jason Reeves, our amazing interior page designer. You make us look good! To Len Evans at Project Publicity, our publicist for helping to introduce this book to the world.

To the MOB Wives of Richmond crew for letting us into your fabulous world: Anelica Mark-Harris, Bessie Mark-Dillard, Arletha Phillips, Christina Harris, Wayne Harris, and Chantennah Spaulding. Special thanks to Anelica for her hospitality and opening up her home to us. To you, Brendan Jordan, for inspiring us with your fierceness and finding time to share your story with us. Thanks to Brendan's mom, Tracy Jordan, for her support of this project as well. To Courtney Constable for sharing your experiences and adventures being a bio-queen. We only wish we could craft drag outfits half as well as you and the Drag Coven do.

To Ryan Caldwell, PhD and Joelle Hawkes, thank you for your valuable support of the book.

To Joanne Brownstein Jarvi for believing in our book concept and making it even better.

To Jen DM and Rick Gradone of Hi Fashion for graciously allowing us to reprint lyrics from our life anthem "Amazing." To Mira Budd, Marcelo Cantu, José Guzmán Colón, Christopher DeVargus, Magnus Hastings, Tina Hodnett, Nick Lovell, Sharon Poole, and Ryan Smith for allowing us to share your wonderful photography with our readers. Thanks to Aman Johnson, my master documentarian, for capturing this whole transformative process.

To our advance readers: Caitlyn Angeloff, Tami Belt, Jennifer DeRuff, Cody Edwards, Jessica Hogue, Beth Jarrett, Katie Kronbergs, Sarah Kronbergs, Ben McCoy, Allison Gibson Montgomery, Nikki Northcutt, Cameron Oefinger, and Jenny Williams; and our advance listener, Butch Smith, thank you for your time and valuable feedback.

....
JACKIE'S ACKNOWLEDGMENTS
....

First, thank you to my collaborator and friend, Shelly
Stewart Kronbergs, for being part of this book project and
supporting it from the very beginning. When I hatched this
wacky idea that drag queens could teach us all to be more
confident, you were the first one to say you loved it. When I
said I was going to do drag myself, you said, "You go girl!"
When I started getting rejection letters from a few agents
and publishers who just didn't get the concept, you told me
to ignore them and keep going. But only when you became
involved in helping write the book did I really believe it was
actually going to happen. Thanks for providing your expertise in psychology, your nurturing support, and your conta-
gious excitement for wanting to help people be better at
being themselves to this project.

Thank you to Rey Lopez for feeding the flames of my
burgeoning love of drag with your monthly drag shows in
San Antonio. Your generosity in supporting this project
from day one has been invaluable. There simply would be no
book without you. Every time I asked you for help, you just
said, "Yes, of course I'll help." And you did. I'm so glad that
we have gotten to experience so many drag adventures
together over the last few years and that I can now call you a
good friend. Thank you for all you do to promote drag in
central Texas with Rey Lopez Entertainment (RLE). You are
bringing not just drag entertainment but joy to so many
people who love the art form. And you've created a family of
like-minded people whose collective bonds were forged
while attending your shows. I'm honored to part of the RLE
family.

Thank you to Kelly Kline, my friend and official drag mother, for your immediate acceptance of me as a woman doing drag. I'm indebted to you for the countless hours of drag mentorship, teaching me everything I need to know to do drag, and doing it with patience and humor. Thank you for soothing my fears and acting as my drag therapist in encouraging me through my moments of self-doubt. You also gave this newbie drag performer a spot in your shows, and I am indebted to you for those opportunities. I couldn't have gotten through the TEDxVancouver performance without your expert guidance. Thank you for your friendship, and all that you do to make our community better with your selfless dedication to charitable and social causes.

To Jaremi Carey (aka Phi Phi O'Hara), thank you for your generosity in helping Lady Trinity come to life. You truly are the Sweetest Bitch! I'm so glad this little TV show about drag could bring us together, and I've had so much fun on our drag adventures. Thank you for your friendship and your support of this as well as my last book. Through you, I've had the pleasure of meeting your amazing partner, Mikhael Mikhol, whom you don't deserve. (Just kidding!) Thank you, Mikhael, for your support and friendship too. I wish I had a drag husband as understanding, loving, and talented with makeup skills and costuming as you are.

Thank you to my drag BFF Cameron Oefinger for loving this art form as much as I do and being right there by my side during this entire wild adventure. Thank you for being part of my performances and my continual cheerleader through it all. You are my one and only drag daughter, and I'm still apologizing for that Halloween contour.

To Bastion Carboni, my first performance coach, thank you for the crash course in acting with those damn monologues and for letting it slide when I was too afraid to do them for you. Thank you for working with me to craft that first seminal number and performing as part of it. Your pep talk that night got me through it. Thank you for your friendship and support. I continued to be inspired by all of your artistic endeavors, including those by Miss Pilar Salt.

Thank you Wendy Sanders (aka Ginger Snaps), the tastiest tease in Texas, for your burlesque mentorship.

Thank you to all of the folks who were part of my drag performances in Austin: Jenny Alperin, Tara Alperin, Vu Doan, Cameron Oefinger, David Urrate, and Colton Wright.

To Irene Scott, stylist extraordinaire, thank you for changing my life. They might be just articles of clothing to some, but for me they were the instruments you used to help this run-of-the-mill dresser become fiercely me. Thank you for your support of this project and for your friendship.

Thank you to all of my TEDxVancouver advisers and crew: Isaiah Harvey, Kelly Kline, Victoria Labalme, Aaron Medina, Barbara Miller, Joel Reynolds, and Quinton Weathers. Thanks also to Shepherd Allen.

Thank you to Seth Godin for being so generous with your advice and support of all of my projects, especially this one.

To Javier Simons, we met through our love of drag, and I'm so happy that we have forged an amazing friendship because of it. Thank you for all of your help with this project. And thank you for always checking in on me to make sure I was okay. With a friend like you, how could I not be?

Thank you to the crew at Oil Can Harry's—Dillon Dority, Danny Lopez, and Dane Smith—for always being so welcoming and supportive of this woman feeling her drag fantasy. Y'all are the best! Thank you to my fellow Austin queens, Cynthia Lee Fontaine, Althea Trix, and Anyzha St. James, who always motivated me to be the best performer I could be by just watching you take creative risks and wow your audiences every time. Thank you to my fellow drag-loving Austin crew who have logged more hours at OCH than we care to count: Anthony Bryan Hilton, Gloria Landron, and Paul Sandoval.

Thank you to my drag costume designers and stylists—Bobby Moffett and those at Lucy in Disguise with Diamonds, the best costume store in the world: Jerry Durham, Emily Hicks, René Newman, and Walter Young.

To Peter Crawford and Pieter van Meeuwen, my drag adventure companions. I've cherished the many adventures we've had over the years, drawn together initially by our common love of drag and poodles. Thank you also for being such ardent supporters of this project and of all that I do. I can't wait for our next adventures together!

Thank you to my RLE family members in San Antonio for your support and friendship: Carrie Auga, Marko Buenrostro, Shaneka Calloway, Richard Herrera, Doug Krantz, Julian Ledezma, and Danielle Stevens. Thank you to the most talented queens in San Antonio for inspiring me with your performances: Tencha La Jefa, along with Toni R. Andrews, Nilaya Milan Raven, and Kristi Waters.

To Derrick Barry, for being such a champion of me as I explored this world of drag. You unconditionally offered your help right off the bat, and I can't tell you how much that has meant to me. Thank you. I also want to thank Derrick's partners, Nick San Pedro and Mackenzie Claude, who are always there with a kind comment and encouraging word every chance they get.

To Jamie Steward Bancroft, thank you for the opportunity to be part of a historic event, the inaugural Austin International Drag Festival. What an amazing thing you are doing for the world of drag and the city of Austin!

To Lyn Christian, Shannon Dee, Jessica Draper, and Virginia Miracle, who were early supporters of this project and were kind enough to pilot workshops based on the book's material.

To Kathryn Ferguson, Todd Hassell, and Rachel Mushahwar for your early support of this work and how these ideas can help women (and men) in the workplace.

Thank you to Barbara Cave McDougal and Rusty Shelton for their early and continued support of the book.

Thank you to my amazing, wonderful friends who always support me in all I do. You inspire me every day with your kindness: Travis Benford, Richard Binhammer, Aaron Bourgeios, Dane Burch, Charles Brown, Don Davis, Walter Davis, Vu Doan, Michael Dobson, Cody Edwards, Elliot Gray Fisher, Jeff Flemings, Julie Foster, Nate Fuentes, Erica Gionfriddo, Stephen Graham, Jerry Kampi, Beckie Lough, Kelly Pierce, Dave Ploof, Jason Reeves, Eric Rodgers, Linda Seals, Anish Shah, Annalisa Perez Shah, Butch Smith, Terry Cotillo Smith, Amy Swank, Kathy Tomasino, Curtis Uhlemann, David Urrate, and Colton Wright.

Thank you to my family for their love and support, as always.

Thank you to RuPaul for elevating the art form of drag to new heights and captivating people around the world. It was you who first inspired me to take on this transformation that started an avalanche of new adventures, new opportunities, and new friends. And it was you who taught all of us the most important lesson of all: "If you can't love yourself, how the hell are you gonna love someone else?"

Can I get an Amen?

SHELLY'S ACKNOWLEDGMENTS

I would like to thank my dear friend and colleague Jackie Huba for inviting me to help write this book. We met after we had both moved into a new condominium in Austin during one of many (false) fire alarms that plagued us that first year. I remember sitting at a table near the pool, introducing myself to her, and learning that she was an author. I was both intrigued and a little envious. It sounded so cool! How did she do that? Could I do that too? Well, eight years, two international trips we took together, two failed relationships under our belts, and many, many happy hours later, I'm grateful that she has mentored me through this process. But I'm even more grateful for my friendship with her, for her support, her kindness, and her no-nonsense approach to the business side of life. She has taught me how to be a kick-ass woman!

Thank you to my friend Lynnae Sorensen, whom I met fifteen years ago at seminary and who never once failed to encourage me, listen to my joys and sorrows, laugh with me, and open a new bottle of wine for me! Thank you to my new Smith family for their acceptance and support: Andrea, Andy, Anne, Blake, Brendon, Dylan, Jerry, Ryan, and Sandy. Thank you to all my friends who have supported me and loved me throughout this process: Kelli Byers, Walter Davis and his husband Stephen Graham, Vu Doan, Julie Foster, Nate Fuentes, Ross Miller (therapist extraordinaire!), Kelly

Pierce and his husband Charles Brown, Bryan Rust, Annalisa Perez Shah and her husband Anish Shah, Molly Van Galen (my soul sister), Cindy Wolf, Colton Wright, and my clients (who shall, of course, remain nameless)—kisses to all of you!

I could not have done this at all without the support of my family. My mother, Pauline Turner; my cousins, especially Valerie Layne; and my three beautiful, fabulous daughters, Katie, Sarah, and Lizzie Kronbergs. Each one of them tells me weekly, and sometimes daily, that they are proud of me, that they know I can do this, and that they love me. I hope with all of my heart that they will continue to be fiercely them, for they are the strong, glorious women I have written about.

Most important, I thank heaven for sending me the man of my dreams—my husband, my soul mate, the love of my life, Butch Smith. He showed up four days after I let the universe know that I was ready for him, and I have been awash in love since that day. Thank you, darling, for your love. It sustains me.

INDEX

Carboni choreographing for, 92; comfort zone pushed for, 55, 139, 142–143, 162; costume of, 62, 136, 159; drag career of, 18; dragercising for, 95–96; drag queens interviewed by, 18; fashion of, 50–56, 56f; fears confronted by, 86–87, 90–91, 137–138, 158–160; fierce realization for, 52, 54–55; first performance of, 92–93, 117–119; inner critic of, 117, 118, 135, 139, 160–161; Kline as drag mother for, 58, 60, 62–63; Kline teaching makeup to, 61; Lady Gaga influencing, 15, 34; Las Vegas event for, 54–55; learning to twirl nipple tassels for, 89–90; Lopez helping, 58; *The Matrix* inspiring, 33; *Monster Loyalty: How Gaga Turns Followers into Fanatics* by, 15–16, 35; naming drag character of, 33–35; parental love and, 63; power and submissiveness in dance of, 93; red lipstick worn by, 54; ruminating by, 139, 161; *RuPaul's Drag Race* inspiring, 16; Scott styling, 51–56, 56f; second drag performance of, 93–94; self-doubt of, 35, 137–139; TEDx rejection for, 157–158; TEDx talk by, 158–160; wig styling for, 61. *See also* Lady Trinity

Huffington Post: "8 Nastiest Reality TV Villains" of the year by, 2

I

"If You're Not Wearing Nails, You're Not Doing Drag," 81

Inthyrath, Airline, 96

J

Jordan, Brendan, 99f; American Apparel campaign for, 100; "Applause" danced to by, 100; criticism toward, 103; Cyrus and, 101; dance video going viral for, 100; "diva kid" as, 100; drag queens inspiring, 102; family of, 101–102; as gender-fluid, 101; great-grandmother as inspiration to, 101–102; invited to *RuPaul's Drag Race*, 100; as LGBT advocate, 103; Marco Marco runway walk by, 100–101; Phi Phi O'Hara doing makeup of, 102; on power of drag, 102; social media of, 100

Judge, Timothy: Bureau of Labor and Statistics report and, 73–74; height and income study by, 73–74

Jujubee, 97f; on confidence, 98; Facebook followers of, 97;

Jujubee, 97f *(continued)*
  Inthyrath drag persona as, 96; nonverbal behaviors of, 97–98; on performance, 97–98; on *RuPaul's Drag Race*, 96–97
Jung, Carl, 42

K
Katya Zamolodchikova, 155
Kline, Kelly, 58; background of, 59–60; in day drag, 59; drag described by, 60; as drag mother, 58, 60, 62–63; drag pageants won by, 59–60; drag show hosted by, 92; fashion and personas of, 59; Huba taught makeup by, 61; Lady Trinity first performance and, 117; wig styling by, 61
Knowles, Beyoncé: background of, 32; in Destiny's Child, 32; Sasha Fierce persona of, 32
Kronbergs, Shelly Stewart, 19; becoming a pastor, 144–146; becoming a psychotherapist, 146; Betty La Belle as stage name for, 147; boudoir photo shoot of, 147; burlesque class for, 146–147; childhood of, 143; education and career of, 19–20, 144–145; on fashion as important, 72; healing process of, 146; on hiding smarts, 143;

marriage of, 144, 146; sexual abuse of, 143, 146; sexuality of, 146, 147–148

L
Lady Gaga: "Applause" by, 100; Huba influenced by, 15, 34; in *Monster Loyalty: How Gaga Turns Followers into Fanatics*, 15–16; music industry impacting, 31; Obama lobbied by, 31; persona of, 31; self-doubt for, 133
Lady Trinity: "Amazing" number performed by, 92–93, 136; asking What Would a Drag Queen Do?, 138; Austin International Drag Festival for, 134–136; costumes of, 62, 136, 159; drag transformation of, 6, 17–18, 60–62; first performance of, 92–93, 117–119; history of, 6, 15; Huba inspired by, 139, 162; Huba naming character of, 33–35; Kline encouraging performance of, 117; Phi Phi O'Hara as drag aunt to, 6; Phi Phi O'Hara styling, 2–3; photo shoot of, 4–6; as powerful woman, 6; preparing for Austin International Drag Festival, 136; qualities of, 33, 35; "Vanity" performance of, 136–139. *See also* Huba, Jackie
Laganja Estranja, 156

Latrice Royale, 63, 64f; drag saving, 64; prison stint for, 64; *on RuPaul's Drag Race*, 64–65; self-confidence of, 64–65; self-love of, 65–66
LGBT rights, 165–166; Cyrus supporting, 101; Happy Hippie Foundation supporting, 101; Jordan advocating for, 103; McCarthy as anti, 165; post World War II violations of, 165; Stonewall Inn riots for, 166
Lolo Brow: criticism of, 124; drag as art form for, 125
"Looking Good and Feeling Gorgeous," 96
Lopez, Rey, 57; Huba learning drag and, 58; queens in drag shows of, 57

M
mansplaining, 42
manspreading, 105; as power move, 111
Marco Marco, 100–101
Mark-Dillard, Bessie, 66f; Beyoncé lip-synced by, 68; birthday party of, 68–69; drag pageant performance of, 69
Mark-Harris, Anelica, 66f, 104; drag brunch of, 68; drag makeover for, 67; drag stylist for Christina hired by, 69–70; on expenses for queens, 71; fortieth birthday party of, 67;

Mark-Dillard as mother of, 68–69; MOB Wives of Richmond leader as, 66. *See also* MOB Wives of Richmond
Matrix, The: Huba inspired by, 33; Moss in, 33–34; Trinity in, 33
McCarthy, Joseph, 165
McCook, Brian: on delusion, 155–156; Katya Zamolod-chikova as drag persona of, 155
Mean Girls, 126
Midler, Bette, 49
Miss Fame, 110; on red lipstick, 80
MOB Wives of Richmond, 66f; chant of, 70; drag shows hosted by, 70–71; Mark-Harris as leader of, 66; Miss MOB Wife title by, 70–71; name of, 66
Monster Loyalty: How Gaga Turns Followers into Fanatics (Huba), 15–16; self-doubt in writing, 35
Moss, Carrie Ann, 33–34

N
negative internalization, 125–126
nipple tassels: learning to twirl, 90; pasties for, 89
nonverbal behaviors: alpha relationships in, 104; dopamine increased by, 106–107; expansive posture as, 105; expressing power through, 94, 99; eye contact as,

transgender drag queens, 24
transvestite, 23
Trixie Mattel, 120f; advice of,
122; childhood of,
120–121; critics of,
122–123; Firkus, Brian as,
119; power in look of, 121;
on *RuPaul's Drag Race*,
121–122; style of, 120
tucking, 58–59

U
Urban Dictionary, 13

V
"Vanity": by Aguilera, 136; Lady
Trinity performing to,
136–139
Victoria Sin, 124
voguing: current forms of, 85;
death drop in, 85; Harlem
drag queens starting, 85;
Madonna borrowing, 85

W
What Would a Drag Queen Do?
(WWDQD), 17; Lady
Trinity "Vanity" perfor-
mance asking, 138;

negative self-talk and,
130; reminders for, 131
wigs: shopping for, 83; styling
of, 61
Williamson, Marianne, 12
Winkle, Helen Van, 38f; Baddie
as persona of, 38; on
Candidly Nicole, 40;
Cosmopolitan title for,
38–39; Cyrus and, 40;
Dimepiece creating ad
with, 40; fashion of, 39–40;
granddaughter photo-
graphing, 39; hardships of,
39; pop stars and, 40; as
rebel, 38; as role model,
40–41; social media of, 39
Wiseman, Rosalind, 126–127
womanspreading, 111
women: confidence study on,
11; as drag feminists, 124;
as female drag queens, 18,
28, 58, 123, 125; gender
parity study of, 11–12;
womanspreading for,
111–112

Y
Yara Sofia, 155

ABOUT THE AUTHORS

JACKIE HUBA

Jackie Huba has spent most of her career challenging people to express the best in themselves. Most recently, she has been helping women build confidence, take risks, and live more fearlessly by harnessing the transformative art of drag. Through her research, she has found that the process drag queens use to transform themselves into bold, female personas for the stage also works to shape the personas we "perform" in everyday life. Jackie discovered this firsthand by creating and performing as a female drag character for the stage, as well as by interviewing many of the world's top drag queens. She has led corporate and public workshops to help women create and explore their own confident and courageous drag characters and channel this fierceness when they need it in everyday situations.

In Jackie's previous work, she challenged marketers to raise the bar on customer relations in her three books on customer loyalty, including the most recent, *Monster Loyalty: How Lady Gaga Turns Followers into Fanatics.* She coined the term "customer evangelism" in her first book, *Creating Customer Evangelists: How Loyal Customers Become a Volunteer Sales Force.* Her second book, *Citizen Marketers: When People Are the Message,* was one of the first books to document the emerging world of social media and how brands should begin to embrace a participatory culture.

In her fifteen years as a professional keynote speaker, she has addressed audiences around the world from the United States to New Zealand, and in Amsterdam, London, Milan, Berlin, and Tokyo. She speaks to thousands of attendees at corporate events for companies such as Disney, Marriott, American Express, Frito-Lay, and American Airlines, as well as at large association conferences. Through her consulting, Jackie has helped leading companies such as Discovery Communications, Whirlpool, Dell, and Kraft to create more loyalty in their customer base.

Jackie is a Forbes.com contributor, and her work has frequently been featured in the media, such as the *Wall Street Journal, New York Times, BusinessWeek,* and *Advertising Age.* She is an eleven-year veteran of IBM and a Pennsylvania State University graduate. Jackie lives in Austin, Texas, where she is head of the Pittsburgh Steelers Fan Club of Austin.

For information on speaking engagements or workshops, visit JackieHuba.com. You can connect with Jackie on social media:

- Twitter: @JackieHuba
- Facebook: Facebook.com/JackieHubaAuthor
- LinkedIn: Linkedin.com/in/JackieHuba
- Instagram: JackieHuba

You can also connect with Lady Trinity on social media:

- Twitter: @LadyTrinity
- Facebook: Facebook.com/LadyTrinityOfficial
- Instagram: TheLadyTrinity

SHELLY STEWART KRONBERGS

Shelly Stewart Kronbergs, MDiv, MA, and LMFT-Associate, has a private psychotherapy practice in Austin, Texas, as a licensed Marriage and Family Therapy Associate. In addition to counseling, she leads workshops for women to help them find purpose and peace, overcome the stresses that block them from their goals, and teach them how family dynamics impact their leadership abilities. She is a graduate of St. Edward's University with a master's degree in counseling. Previously, she was an ordained pastor in the Evangelical Lutheran Church in America and also holds a master's degree in divinity from the Seminary of the Southwest. Her undergraduate degree is from the University of Texas at Austin, where she was proud to be a member of Alpha Xi Delta.

The mother of three daughters, a happy new bride, an avid reader, a decent crafter, and a mediocre cook, she understands that her main purpose in life is to let people know they are loved and have nothing to fear.

For more information on Shelly's counseling practice, visit here2love.com. You can also connect with Shelly on Facebook at Facebook.com/ShellyStewartKronbergs and on LinkedIn at Linkedin.com/in/ShellyStewartKronbergs.

Berrett–Koehler
Publishers

Berrett-Koehler is an independent publisher dedicated to an ambitious mission: *connecting people and ideas to create a world that works for all.*

We believe that to truly create a better world, action is needed at all levels—individual, organizational, and societal. At the individual level, our publications help people align their lives with their values and with their aspirations for a better world. At the organizational level, our publications promote progressive leadership and management practices, socially responsible approaches to business, and humane and effective organizations. At the societal level, our publications advance social and economic justice, shared prosperity, sustainability, and new solutions to national and global issues.

A major theme of our publications is "Opening Up New Space." Berrett-Koehler titles challenge conventional thinking, introduce new ideas, and foster positive change. Their common quest is changing the underlying beliefs, mindsets, institutions, and structures that keep generating the same cycles of problems, no matter who our leaders are or what improvement programs we adopt.

We strive to practice what we preach—to operate our publishing company in line with the ideas in our books. At the core of our approach is stewardship, which we define as a deep sense of responsibility to administer the company for the benefit of all of our "stakeholder" groups: authors, customers, employees, investors, service providers, and the communities and environment around us.

We are grateful to the thousands of readers, authors, and other friends of the company who consider themselves to be part of the "BK Community." We hope that you, too, will join us in our mission.

A BK Life Book

This book is part of our BK Life series. BK Life books change people's lives. They help individuals improve their lives in ways that are beneficial for the families, organizations, communities, nations, and world in which they live and work. To find out more, visit **www.bk-life.com**.

Berrett–Koehler
Publishers

Connecting people and ideas
to create a world that works for all

Dear Reader,

Thank you for picking up this book and joining our worldwide community of Berrett-Koehler readers. We share ideas that bring positive change into people's lives, organizations, and society.

To welcome you, we'd like to offer you a free e-book. You can pick from among twelve of our bestselling books by entering the promotional code **BKP92E** here: http://www.bkconnection.com/welcome.

When you claim your free e-book, we'll also send you a copy of our e-newsletter, the *BK Communiqué*. Although you're free to unsubscribe, there are many benefits to sticking around. In every issue of our newsletter you'll find

- A free e-book
- Tips from famous authors
- Discounts on spotlight titles
- Hilarious insider publishing news
- A chance to win a prize for answering a riddle

Best of all, our readers tell us, "Your newsletter is the only one I actually read." So claim your gift today, and please stay in touch!

Sincerely,

Charlotte Ashlock
Steward of the BK Website

Questions? Comments? Contact me at bkcommunity@bkpub.com.

MIX
Paper from
responsible sources
FSC® C011935
www.fsc.org
FSC

Certified

B

Corporation
bcorporation.net